ROASTING

PAN

SUPPERS

ROASTING

PAN

SUPPERS

ROSIE SYKES

First published in the United Kingdom in 2020 by
National Trust Books
43 Great Ormond Street
London WC1N 3HZ
An imprint of Pavilion Books Company Ltd

ISBN: 9781911358855

A CIP catalogue record for this book is available from the British Library.

25 24 23 22 21 20
10 9 8 7 6 5 4 3 2 1

Reproduction by Rival Colour Ltd, UK
Printed by Toppan Leefung Ltd, China

This book is available at National Trust shops and online
at www.nationaltrustbooks.co.uk, or try the publisher
(www.pavilionbooks.com) or your local bookshop.

NOTES

- Medium, free-range eggs are used unless otherwise specified. Warning:
  recipes containing raw eggs are unsuitable for pregnant women or
  young children.
- Reasonable care has been taken to ensure the accuracy of the recipes and
  instructions in this book. However, any liability for inaccuracies or errors
  relating to the material contained within the book is expressly excluded to
  the fullest extent permitted by law.
- You may not always achieve the desired results. Oven temperatures vary
  between different appliances and different equipment may affect the desired
  outcome. Neither the National Trust, National Trust (Enterprises) Ltd nor
  Pavilion Books Ltd accept any responsibility or liability for the end results
  of the recipes featured in this book.

INTRODUCTION

As a chef of 20-odd years standing, I have spent much time in front of a range, slinging about pans of all shapes and sizes. In the professional kitchen, the oven was really the domain of the pastry section. Yet during the times of day when I was doing my mise en place – i.e. getting ready for the hustle and bustle of service – I sometimes cooked things in the oven when space on the range was at a premium. The all-round heat of the oven is easier to manage than the direct heat of the hob. A roasting pan just requires a shake now and again, whereas a saucepan needs frequent stirring to prevent ingredients from sticking or burning.

As I used the oven more and more, experimenting and learning, I started thinking of various tricks and techniques – for example, thickening up a tomato sauce or making a chutney works really well in the oven. (One of my favourite lessons from writing this book was perfecting the art of the tomato sauce in the oven – the recipe is in the Fish chapter, on page 50.) And so this book was born. I have included flavours from all over the world, to make this an even more interesting culinary journey. I also always aim to cook as sustainably as possible. Nowadays, you can easily pick up affordable, environmentally-friendly alternatives to common kitchenware, such as reusable kitchen towels instead of kitchen paper and beeswax wraps instead of clingfilm.

This kind of cooking is not an exact science: there are just a few basic principles, and it's a great way to build your confidence in the kitchen. Hopefully you'll end up with a repertoire of personal favourites that you make and share again and again.

I've discovered a few things that add value to the experience, chiefly that it is worth having roasting pans in various sizes (especially as a few of the recipes call for more than one roasting pan). Most of the dishes in the book respond very well to being cooked in metal, but ceramic or ovenproof glass baking dishes will work too. The roasting pans I use most – and these are approximate sizes – are:

SMALL: 30 X 20CM

MEDIUM: 35 X 25CM

LARGE: 40 X 30CM

In some recipes I have suggested which size to use, but it may depend on the result you are looking for. Some good pointers are:

• When roasting pieces of meat, and to some extent fish and vegetables, spread them out so that they can cook evenly all over and caramelise a bit – this part of the process contributes rich flavours.

• Select a tray with enough space for the heat to circulate. This will ensure you don't create steam, which is the enemy of crispness. This is important when cooking chicken thighs with their skin on, for example, as you want to get a nice crisp skin.

• As a general rule, a larger surface area will yield a drier result. So if you are trying to thicken a sauce and reduce some juices, go for a bigger pan.

• When braising meat, packing it together in a huddle once it has been browned will help to keep moisture in and make for a more succulent, tender final product.

• When softening vegetables, especially onions, a smaller surface area is preferable. Always add a pinch of salt at the beginning as this helps them break down and release moisture, and in turn steam and soften.

• Most baking works best in a small or medium pan, unless you are going for a whopper cake, in which case you will need to scale up quantities.

I find that many great dishes begin with an onion or something else in that family. Consequently, many of the recipes start with sweating onions in a roasting pan. This works extremely well in the oven and, although it requires patience, it doesn't need constant attention, as it would if cooking in a pan on the hob. The even temperature and steamy environment means they are less likely to stick; a stir now and again is a good idea, but generally if left to their own devices the result will be sweet and rich, which is what a good base flavour relies on.

Most vegetables respond very well to roasting. I occasionally suggest giving them a few minutes in boiling salted water first, otherwise they may dry out too much. Everything else is possible in a roasting pan in the oven.

COOKING MEAT AND FISH

The oven is traditionally home to big pieces of meat, such as hearty roasts and braises, or slow-cooked stews. However, it is also a very efficient way to cook smaller pieces of meat, such as chops and steaks, pieces of chicken, or sausages, especially if your vegetables are cooked in the same pan. You will find plenty of recipes that can be on the table in under an hour from start to finish, along with a few slow cookers, which would be great for weekends when time is not of the essence (see Timing Is Everything, page 10).

Aim always to buy meat with the highest possible welfare standards: eating less meat of higher quality is more environmentally sustainable in the long term. If you have the time, I would encourage you to chat to your local butcher, who may have some interesting pearls of wisdom. When buying fish, look for sustainably sourced fish, which will display the Marine Stewardship Council (MSC) logo (for more information see the Marine Conservation Society website mcsuk.org).

Fish takes less time to cook than meat because its muscle structure is completely different and heat can permeate the flesh much more quickly. Cooking times depend on a variety of factors – the type of fish, the thickness of the pieces used, and whether or not they are on the bone – but it is important not to overcook fish. Perfectly cooked fish becomes opaque and flakes easily. If cooked with its skin, you will know it is ready when the skin peels off with ease.

A number of the recipes in this chapter call for skinless firm white fish. I tend not to specify more than that because it really depends on what is available. If you are lucky enough to have a local fishmonger, take guidance from them and ask them to do all the filleting, skinning and boning – they will have the knives and the skill to do this efficiently.

MAKING THE MOST OF VEGETABLES

Having dedicated most of our time to preparing the meat or fish, we often find ourselves turning out the same old thing to have alongside our supper, and side dishes become something of a safe, predictable afterthought. There is nothing wrong with this – I am a big fan of frozen peas, as is my dachshund – but it's good to expand your repertoire with some simple, flavoursome side dishes that you can bung in the oven. Several of these dishes would also group together as a feast in themselves (see Cooking Up a Feast, page 12). I have included quite a few vegan recipes and others are fairly easy to turn vegan with the substitution or omission of dairy.

Britain is truly lucky to have a great array of vegetables available. Look for the Red Tractor logo – the Union Flag in the logo indicates the food has been farmed, processed and packed in the United Kingdom. While it is wonderful to grow our own or visit farmers' markets and farm shops, often there just isn't the time. Some supermarkets have local producers on board, or sell the less-than-perfect veg which, at one time, wouldn't have made it onto their shelves. Choose organic produce whenever possible – look for the Soil Association logo. Organic farming avoids the use of synthetic pesticides, herbicides and fertilisers, so it's better for the environment and better for us. I try and cook seasonally as much as I can and have put together vegetables that generally are picked around the same time of year. That said, frozen vegetables and tinned pulses are a boon for a busy lifestyle.

SWEET

According to current culinary trends, it seems that puddings are increasingly restricted to entertaining rather than the traditional end of an everyday meal. However, a sweet treat now and again is always welcome. Pears, plums, peaches, apricots and figs all respond well to oven-roasting, with the addition of cream, thick Greek-style yoghurt, custard or ice cream and a crisp biscuit. And they may just as easily find their way into a bowl of porridge for breakfast or as the filling for a cake or pie. This chapter includes a range of simple-to-prepare recipes for puddings that work equally well for elevenses or tea.

I am a firm believer that recipes are a framework; once you are in the zone, modification comes easily and then a recipe truly becomes your own. So use this collection as a springboard for your own creativity. Happy roasting pan cooking!

TIMING IS EVERYTHING

Sometimes speed is of the essence: here is an idea of what can be on the table hastily or at a more leisurely pace. The 30-minute column includes a few enticing sides which would be great with some grilled sausages or bacon, or simply cooked fish. The longer receipes don't require you to be hands-on for anywhere near the amount of time stated – the ingredients do their own thing in the oven while you do the same elsewhere!

ABOUT 30 MINUTES

- Lamb steaks in mojo verde with roast potatoes and green pepper
  (see page 47)

- Pork tenderloin and lemon cauliflower
  (see page 31)

- Roast cauliflower and broccoli with toasted almond dressing
  (VEGAN) (see page 125)

- Whole roast mackerel and spring onions with tarragon
  (see page 65)

- Fish wrapped in ham with butter beans and sun-dried tomatoes
  (see page 68)

- Roast asparagus with egg toasts
  (see page 86)

UNDER AN HOUR

- Duck breast with pot-roast chicory and celeriac
  (see page 27)

- Tom's sausages and beans
  (see page 28)

- Pork chops baked with fennel, tomato and potato
  (see page 32)

- Easy moussaka
  (see page 40)

- Yoghurt-baked fish with chilli sweet potato and peanut chutney
  (see page 55)

- Smoked haddock, broccoli and farfalle
  (see page 51)

- Green couscous with prawns
  (see page 61)

- Spiced white fish with noodles and broth
  (see page 62)

- Fancy fish fingers and beans
  (see page 66)

- Cod, orzo, sweet potato and tapenade
  (see page 70)

- Plaice baked with fennel, potatoes and cider
  (see page 67)

- Spinach, walnut and feta in the hole
  (see page 82)

- Pea and artichoke risotto
  (see page 84)

- Vicky's filo pie
  (see page 89)

- Baked angel hair pasta with broccoli and green beans
  (VEGAN) (see page 90)

- Farinata, red pepper and courgette with olive dressing
  (VEGAN) (see page 93)

- Cauliflower kuku
  (see page 94)

- French onion Welsh rarebit
  (see page 96)

- Rice pudding with a difference
  (see page 130)

- Marmalade baked pears (VEGAN)
  (see page 133)

- Baked rhubarb, rose water and pink grapefruit
  (VEGAN) (see page 134)

1 HOUR

OVER AN HOUR

COOKING UP A FEAST

Most of the roasting pan suppers are a whole meal in themselves, but it is easy to add a side dish and sweet thing when having friends over. We have put together some meal plans to make entertaining a breeze. The book has an array of dishes from around the world, so we have picked flavours that compliment each other. For pudding, a bit of cream, creme fraiche or sorbet never goes amiss.

FEAST WITH FRIENDS

LAIDBACK, WITH TIME TO COOK

- Beef chilli with cornbread top
  (see page 36)

- Roast celeriac with wholegrain mustard and rosemary
  (see page 110)

- *A simple green salad to serve*

- Baked rhubarb, rose water and pink grapefruit
  (see page 134)
  add double cream, Greek yoghurt or mascarpone with a biscuit

PREPARE IN ADVANCE

- Aromatic chicken with almonds
  (see page 16)

- Roasted okra
  (see page 110)

- Baked baby carrots and harissa
  (see page 116)

- *Flatbreads, naan or parathas would go well with the above*

- Rice pudding with a difference
  (see page 130)
  served with oven-baked fruit or a dried fruit compote

A TABLE OF GOODIES

THESE DISHES WORK WELL
TOGETHER IF YOU ARE PLANNING
A BIG PARTY WITH PEOPLE HELPING
THEMSELVES FROM THE TABLE

- Miso aubergine and togarashi chicken skewers
  (see page 24)

- Dawn's slow-cooked shoulder of lamb with Chinese pancakes
  (see page 42)

- Charred cabbage with chilli and sherry vinegar
  (see page 108)

- Broccoli 'rice', flageolet beans and roast vegetables
  (see page 111)

- Marmalade baked pears
  (see page 133)
  served with cream or ice cream and some simple biscuits

AL FRESCO

- Jerk chicken strips, black rice and black eye beans
  (see page 22)

- Baked angel hair pasta with broccoli and green beans
  (see page 90)

- Roast cauliflower and broccoli with toasted almond dressing
  (see page 125)

- Apricot and pistachio tart
  (see page 141)

QUICK AND MESSY MIDWEEK SUPPER

- Baked mussels with tomato and fregola
  (see page 52)

- Roast cauliflower and broccoli with toasted almond dressing
  (see page 125)

- *A crunchy cucumber and dill salad to serve*

- Chocolate banana tahini brownie
  (see page 128)
  crème fraîche or yoghurt ice cream will add a nice sharp note to the rich pudding

VEGGIE TREATS

LAIDBACK, WITH TIME TO COOK

- Spinach, walnut and feta in the hole (see page 82)

- Baby baked carrots and harissa (see page 116)

- Rhubarb, pistachio and ginger cake (see page 136) *pouring cream or crème fraîche never goes amiss when serving this as pudding*

MIDWEEK SUPPER

- Pea and artichoke risotto (see page 84)

- Charred cabbage with chilli and sherry vinegar (see page 108)

- Raspberry and sour cream squares (see page 138)

QUICK AND EASY

- Roast asparagus with egg toasts (see page 86)

- Oven-baked mushrooms à la grecque (see page 124)

- *Sometimes a pudding just isn't on the cards – some cheese and fresh fruit is just as good*

VEGAN FEAST

RELAXED COOKING TIME

- Baked pearl barley, peas, beans and green sauce (see page 102)

- Baked beetroot with hazelnut dressing (see page 113)

- Baked rhubarb, rose water and pink grapefruit (see page 134)

PREPARE IN ADVANCE

- Red peppers stuffed with spiced chickpeas and aubergine (see page 81)

- Potato and tomato gratin (for a vegan version, substitute the butter for more oil and instead of Parmesan use panko breadcrumbs) (see page 120)

- Walnut, pecan and date squares (for a vegan version, omit the eggs) (see page 140)

QUICK SUPPER

- Broccoli 'rice', flageolet beans and roast vegetables (see page 111)

- Charred cabbage with chilli and sherry vinegar (see page 108)

- Marmalade baked pears (see page 133)

CELEBRATION MEALS

MEAT

- Rice baked with crab, peas and broccoli (see page 56)

- Minted roast chicken with potatoes, peas and lettuce (see page 17)

- Baked roots with Lancashire cheese crumbs (see page 114)

- Walnut, pecan and date squares (see page 140)

FISH

- Cauliflower kuku (see page 94)

- Ana's fish parcels (see page 72)

- Tomato and pepper tian (see page 97)

- Rhubarb, pistachio and ginger cake (see page 136)

VEGGIE

- Baked farinata, red pepper and courgette with olive dressing (see page 93)

- Vicky's filo pie (see page 89)

- Roast celeriac with wholegrain mustard and rosemary (see page 110)

- Marmalade baked pears (see page 133)

MEAT

AROMATIC CHICKEN WITH ALMONDS

This lovely gentle curry comes from my sister – it is a firm favourite in her household. If you plan ahead, you can rub the chicken with lemon and salt and leave it overnight – this has a tenderising effect on the meat.

SERVES 4

8 boneless skinless
   chicken thighs
Juice of ½ lemon
2 teaspoons salt
30g flaked almonds
3 tablespoons sunflower
   or rapeseed oil
3 onions, finely sliced
5 large cloves garlic,
   finely grated or crushed
4cm thumb of ginger,
   peeled and grated
20g butter
1 cinnamon stick
5 black or 10 green
   cardamom pods
8 cloves
3 teaspoons ground
   cumin
3 teaspoons ground
   coriander
2 teaspoons turmeric
1–2 teaspoons cayenne
   pepper
120g ground almonds
300g passata
500g boiling water
Generous handful of
   coriander, chopped

Prick the chicken all over with a fork and rub with the lemon juice and salt. Set aside for at least 30 minutes or overnight.

Preheat the oven to 190°C (170°C fan), gas mark 5. Put the flaked almonds in a roasting pan and put them into the oven to toast gently as the oven heats up. Keep a close eye on the nuts as you want them to be just golden. Once the almonds are toasted, tip them into a bowl and set aside.

Add the oil to the hot roasting pan, then add the onions and a pinch of salt and place in the oven for about 15 minutes until they are light brown, stirring halfway through.

Add the garlic, ginger and butter and cook for 7 minutes, shaking halfway through. Add the whole spices and toast in the oven for a few minutes. Finally add the ground spices and return to the oven for a few minutes. Stir in the ground almonds until you have a smooth thick paste, then add the passata and the boiling water and return to the oven until the mixture is simmering, which should take 5–10 minutes.

Once the sauce is bubbling, add the chicken thighs and cook for about 30 minutes, checking after 20 minutes and adding a little more boiling water if most of the liquid has evaporated.

Once the chicken is cooked through, leave it to sit for a good 15 minutes before serving – you can do this in the cooling oven with the door ajar. Scatter over the chopped coriander and toasted flaked almonds to serve.

I like to serve this with naan breads or paratha and roasted okra (page 110).

MINTED ROAST CHICKEN WITH POTATOES, PEAS AND LETTUCE

Mint sauce is the secret weapon in this dish. If I have any other soft herbs knocking around I will add them to the mint sauce – tarragon and parsley are favourites as they make this into a very simple salsa verde.

SERVES 4

1 whole chicken,
   approx. 1.5kg
2 generous tablespoons
   mint sauce
1 tablespoon sunflower
   or rapeseed oil
320g new potatoes,
   cut in half
30g butter
2 Little Gem lettuce,
   outer leaves removed,
   cut into four or six,
   lengthways
6 spring onions, cut
   into 4cm lengths
400ml boiling chicken
   stock
200g frozen peas,
   defrosted
Sea salt and black pepper

Season the chicken generously all over and rub with the mint sauce – you can do this several hours in advance or even the night before if you like. The chicken needs to be at room temperature before it goes into the oven, so take it out of the fridge and set aside for an hour or two before cooking.

Preheat the oven to 200°C (180°C fan), gas mark 6.

Put the oil into the roasting pan, add the potatoes and stir them about to coat them with the oil. Season the potatoes then sit the chicken on top, dot it all over with the butter and grind over some black pepper. Put the pan into the oven and roast for 20 minutes.

Turn the oven down to 180°C (160°C fan), gas mark 4, and cook for another 15 minutes.

Snuggle the lettuce in among the potatoes and cook for 15 minutes until it starts to soften. Add the spring onions and hot stock and return to the oven for 15 minutes.

To check that the chicken is cooked, pierce the thickest part of the thigh with a skewer: the juices should run clear, with no hint of pink. When the chicken is cooked through, lift it out and leave to rest in a warm place.

Add the peas to the roasting pan and put back in the oven for 15 minutes. If there's a lot of liquid surrounding the vegetables, turn the oven up to 200°C (180°C fan), gas mark 6, to help the liquid reduce while the peas cook.

Cut up the chicken and serve with the vegetables and the lovely juices.

GINGER AND TURMERIC CHICKEN WITH POTATO AND CHICKPEA CURRY

The chicken can be rubbed with the spice paste up to 24 hours in advance to intensify the flavours. This recipe would also work well with a firm fish fillet – simply add the fish nearer the end of the cooking time.

SERVES 4

Small handful of
    coriander, roughly
    chopped, including
    the stalks, plus
    extra to serve
4cm thumb of ginger,
    wiped clean and
    roughly chopped
1 tablespoon turmeric
½ teaspoon sea salt
Grated zest and juice
    of 1 lime
1 tablespoon light
    olive oil
8 chicken thighs, skin on

Put the coriander, ginger, turmeric, salt, lime zest and juice into a food processor or large pestle and mortar. Grind to a smooth paste that will coat the meat, gradually adding the oil to help the process. Rub the chicken with the ginger/turmeric mix and set aside in a dish for as long as you can – ideally up to 24 hours.

Preheat the oven to 190°C (170°C fan), gas mark 5, and put a roasting pan in to heat up.

To make the curry, put the seeds and dry spices into the hot roasting pan, shaking the pan until they start to release their aroma. Put the pan back into the oven for a minute. When you take it out again, add the chickpeas, potatoes, onions, tomatoes, olive oil, tamarind paste and brown sugar, then add the boiling water and mix everything together very thoroughly. Sprinkle with salt and place the chicken thighs on top, skin-side up, spaced apart so that the skin can crisp up all over. Rub or brush the thighs with any marinade that has gathered in the dish. Roast for about 30 minutes and then give everything a good shake and add a little more boiling water if it seems dry.

Return to the oven for another 20–30 minutes.

FOR THE CURRY

½ tablespoon nigella
  seeds
1½ teaspoons smoked
  paprika
1 tablespoon ground
  cumin
¾ tablespoon ground
  coriander
400g tin chickpeas,
  drained and rinsed
8 new potatoes, cut
  in half lengthways
2 red onions, cut in half
  and then into wedges
12 small tomatoes, cut
  in half – I like the
  little plum ones
2 tablespoons light
  olive oil
1 tablespoon
  tamarind paste
1 teaspoon light
  brown sugar
250ml boiling water
Sea salt

After this time the chicken should have crisp, golden skin. Test the potatoes with a thin knife blade or skewer: if they aren't cooked through, cook for another 10 minutes.

If there doesn't seem to be enough curry sauce, use a slotted spoon to transfer the chicken to a warm serving dish, then add some boiling water to the roasting pan with the potato/chickpea mixture and stir vigorously, scraping up any tasty bits. Return the pan to the oven and let the sauce reduce for a few minutes until you have lovely saucy curry to serve with the chicken thighs. Scatter over some chopped coriander to serve.

TIP Although recipes often suggest peeling the ginger, a wise friend of mine suggested it really isn't necessary so long as it has been wiped clean – the skin contains good flavour and if it is being whizzed up in a paste it works perfectly.

SATAY CHICKEN WINGS AND RICE NOODLE SALAD

Satay is a real winner with adults and children alike. This dish is a fun one to have as it requires lots of finger licking and getting down and dirty!

SERVES 4

140g crunchy
  peanut butter
125ml coconut milk
2 red chillies, deseeded
  and chopped
2 tablespoons fish sauce
1 tablespoon soy sauce
Grated zest and juice
  of 1 lime
1.2kg chicken wings, tips
  removed and cut in
  half at the joint
Sea salt and black pepper

FOR THE NOODLE SALAD

80g cashew nuts, roughly
  chopped
200g rice noodles
1 small cucumber
2 carrots
1 bunch of spring
  onions, chopped
1 red chilli, deseeded
  and finely chopped
Small handful of
  coriander, chopped
3 tablespoons sesame oil
2 tablespoons sherry
  vinegar

Put the peanut butter, coconut milk, chillies, fish sauce, soy sauce and lime zest and juice in a food processor and whizz until just combined; don't overdo it if you want some texture from the peanuts. Set aside some of the sauce to use for dipping – about 1 tablespoon per person.

Put the chicken wings in a bowl, add the peanut sauce and toss to coat thoroughly. Set aside for at least 30 minutes or overnight in the fridge. Remember to take the wings out of the fridge 30 minutes before cooking.

Preheat the oven to 220°C (200°C fan), gas mark 7. Put the cashews in a roasting pan and put them in the oven to toast as the oven heats up. Keep a sharp eye on the nuts they can burn very quickly. Tip them into a bowl and set aside.

Put the wings in the hot roasting pan in a single layer, season and bake for 25–30 minutes, turning halfway through. If a lot of liquid is gathering in the pan, tip it out.

While the wings are cooking, make the salad. Cook the rice noodles as directed on the pack and refresh in cold water. Use a vegetable peeler to cut the cucumber and peeled carrot into long strips. Mix the noodles with the cucumber, carrots and the remaining ingredients, including half the toasted cashews. Scatter the remaining cashews over the top.

Serve the wings with any pan juices in a bowl to spoon over, alongside the salad and the peanut sauce for dipping.

JERK CHICKEN STRIPS, BAKED RICE AND BLACK EYE BEANS

This is my version of a Jamaican jerk seasoning. I have suggested using chicken breasts here, but I have also cooked a whole roast chicken in this way.

SERVES 4

3 large skinless chicken breasts, sliced into 3cm strips

1 tablespoon sunflower oil

FOR THE JERK MARINADE

3 teaspoons ground allspice

1 teaspoon ground black pepper

½ teaspoon ground cinnamon

½ teaspoon nutmeg

½ tablespoon dried thyme

5 spring onions, sliced, using as much of the green part as possible

2 Scotch bonnet chillies, chopped (remove the seeds if you don't like it too hot)

1 tablespoon soft dark brown sugar

2 tablespoons dark soy sauce

Juice of 1 lime

1 teaspoon salt

For the jerk marinade, put everything into a food processor and whizz to a smooth paste: it may take a while, but don't be tempted to add water as you want a good thick paste. Taste and add more seasoning if necessary, and an extra chilli if you like it hot. Rub the marinade into the chicken pieces, cover and leave for at least 30 minutes or up to 4 hours.

To prepare the rice, preheat the oven to 200°C (180°C fan), gas mark 6. Put a roasting pan into the oven with the oil. Once hot, add the lardons and onion and a good pinch of salt and cook for 15 minutes, stirring halfway through.

Add the garlic, dried chilli and thyme and return to the oven for a few minutes. Stir in the rice, ensuring it gets well coated. Add the coconut milk, stock and a good pinch of salt, cover the roasting pan with foil and cook for 25 minutes. Check how the rice is doing: if it is nearly tender and there's a lot of liquid, remove the foil – or you may want to keep it covered. Add the beans and return to the oven for 7 minutes.

FOR THE RICE AND BEANS

1 tablespoon
    sunflower oil
100g lardons
1 large onion, sliced
2 cloves garlic, crushed
1 whole dried chilli
Couple of sprigs
    of thyme
300g long grain rice,
    washed until the
    water runs clear
330ml coconut milk
200ml boiling chicken
    or vegetable stock
400g tin black eye beans,
    drained and rinsed
1 tablespoon butter
Small handful of chopped
    coriander
Sea salt and black pepper

About halfway through the rice cooking time, put another roasting pan into the oven for the chicken, adding the oil – if you have a ridged pan this would be excellent. After 5–7 minutes the pan should be good and hot; add the chicken strips and spread out in a single layer. Cook for 10 minutes, shaking the pan halfway through.

When the rice is cooked, take it out of the oven, stir in the butter and try to pick out the thyme stalks and whole chilli. Let it sit for 5 minutes.

Check that the chicken is cooked through and let it rest for a couple of minutes, then serve atop a pile of rice.

MISO AUBERGINE AND TOGARASHI CHICKEN SKEWERS

This recipe draws on a few Japanese influences. The 'yakitori' – little marinated chicken skewers – are marinated with togarashi seasoning, popular in Japan, where it is often added to ramen noodle dishes.

SERVES 2

FOR THE AUBERGINES

2 smallish aubergines
2 teaspoons sunflower oil
5 teaspoons white miso paste
1 teaspoon fruity olive oil
3cm thumb of ginger, peeled and finely grated
1 tablespoon soy sauce
1 teaspoon honey
1 teaspoon Tabasco, or less if you are not so keen on hot stuff

FOR THE CHICKEN

Juice of 1 orange
1 teaspoon soy sauce
1 clove garlic, finely grated or crushed
1 teaspoon sunflower oil
1½ teaspoons togarashi
2 skinless chicken breasts, sliced into long strips, about 2cm wide
Spring onions, sliced, to garnish

Preheat the oven to 190°C (170°C fan), gas mark 5. If you are using wooden skewers, soak them in cold water.

Slice the aubergines in half lengthways, leaving their stalks on. Cut some slashes into the flesh, about halfway through. Rub the aubergines all over with 1 teaspoon of the sunflower oil and set them flesh-side down in a roasting pan. Cover with foil and place in the oven for 20 minutes.

Meanwhile, make the aubergine marinade: in a mixing bowl, whisk together the miso paste, the remaining sunflower oil, olive oil, grated ginger, soy sauce, honey and Tabasco. Take all but a tablespoon of this mixture out of the bowl and set aside.

Make the chicken marinade in the bowl with the tablespoon of miso mixture: add the orange juice, soy sauce, garlic, oil and togarashi. Toss the chicken in the marinade and set aside.

Turn the aubergines over, cover with foil and bake for another 15–20 minutes until soft.

Turn the oven up to its highest setting: 220°C (200°C fan), gas mark 7. Divide the miso mixture between the aubergines and smear it all over the flesh. Return to the oven for a couple of minutes while you thread the marinated chicken onto the skewers, reserving the marinade.

Take the roasting pan with the aubergines out of the oven. Place the chicken skewers next to the aubergines and pour the reserved marinade over the meat. Return to the oven for 5 minutes, then check the chicken. If necessary, turn the skewers over and give it another 5 minutes or so.

Sprinkle over the sliced spring onions and serve with sticky rice.

DUCK BREAST WITH POT-ROAST CHICORY AND CELERIAC

I found cooked chicory to be a revelation the first time I tried it: it becomes soft and loses some of the bitterness. Along with the sweetness of the shallots and apple and the earthiness of the celeriac, it is the perfect foil for duck.

SERVES 4

2 large duck breasts
  or 3 smaller ones,
  trimmed of any
  sinew, fat scored in
  a criss-cross
Splash of sunflower
  or rapeseed oil
6 large banana shallots,
  sliced in half
  lengthways
1 large celeriac, approx
  1.4kg, peeled and cut
  into 2cm wide chips
3 heads of white chicory,
  cut in half lengthways
2 bay leaves
3 tablespoons sherry
  vinegar
100ml boiling vegetable
  or chicken stock
2 apples, cored and each
  cut into eight wedges
Sea salt and black pepper

Preheat the oven to 220°C (200°C fan), gas mark 7, and put a large roasting pan in to heat up.

Rub a good pinch of salt into the scored fat of each duck breast and a little onto the flesh too. Season both sides with a good grinding of pepper.

Once the roasting pan is hot, take it out of the oven, add the oil and the duck breasts, skin-side down. They should sizzle as they go in. Put them into the oven for 10 minutes until the skin becomes crisp and brown and renders out some fat. Halfway through, pour off any fat (reserve this for later). Turn the breasts over and roast for 3 minutes to brown the flesh side. Once browned all over, lift the duck out of the roasting pan and set aside. You need about 2½ tablespoons of fat, so if necessary add a little of the fat you poured off earlier.

Now add the shallots, celeriac, chicory and bay leaves, season generously and stir everything about until well coated with the duck fat. Place in the oven until starting to soften, about 15 minutes.

Throw in the sherry vinegar and return the pan to the oven until it has almost completely evaporated. Then add the stock and apples and give everything a good shake. Sit the duck breasts on top of the vegetables and return to the oven for 5 minutes.

I usually cook the duck breasts until they are pink but not bloody: to test, if you press your chin, then press the flesh side of the duck, that is the consistency you are looking for. Remove the duck and leave to rest.

Give the vegetables 10 minutes more in the oven, until tender and loosely coated with the stock. Slice the duck and serve atop the vegetable mixture. I might serve some watercress and redcurrant jelly alongside.

TOM'S SAUSAGES AND BEANS

Tom is a great friend and an excellent cook. This dish is very simple and the secret here is that the beans shouldn't be in too much liquid by the end – they should have a certain unctuousness about them.

SERVES 2

75g smoked pancetta,
  cut into small cubes
4 best-quality pork
  sausages
2 teaspoons duck fat,
  lard or sunflower oil
  (if needed)
125g banana shallots,
  cut into 2–3cm thick
  rounds
1 carrot, diced
1 celery stick, diced
6 large cloves garlic,
  crushed or grated
400g tin flageolet beans,
  drained and rinsed
200ml boiling chicken
  or vegetable stock
Small handful of parsley,
  chopped
Sea salt and black pepper

Preheat the oven to 200°C (180°C fan), gas mark 6, and put a roasting pan in to heat up.

Once hot, add the pancetta and sausages and place in the oven for about 10 minutes until the sausages brown and the pancetta cubes render down, shaking the pan halfway through. Remove the sausages and set aside.

If the pancetta has not rendered much fat, add a couple of teaspoons of fat or oil. Add the shallots, carrot and celery and stir well to coat with the fat, add a good pinch of salt and return to the oven for 7–10 minutes until everything starts to soften. A little bit of colour is fine but if it is looking too brown, cover with foil.

Add the garlic and beans and stir thoroughly, then pour in the stock and return to the oven for 10–15 minutes so that all the flavours combine.

Add the parsley and give the beans a stir. Taste for seasoning. Pop the sausages on top of the beans and return to the oven for 5–7 minutes to heat through. Serve with lashings of English mustard.

PORK TENDERLOIN AND LEMON CAULIFLOWER

In this recipe I suggest using two roasting pans – the cauliflower is so much nicer when spread out, as it gets lovely caramelised crispy edges. The roasted cauliflower also makes an ideal vegan main course.

SERVES 4

2 teaspoons coriander
seeds
1½ teaspoons fennel seeds
¾ teaspoon ground ginger
¾ teaspoon smoked
paprika
½ teaspoon sea salt
1 teaspoon dried thyme
1 sprig each of sage
and rosemary, leaves
chopped
2 tablespoons honey
Zest and juice of ½ lemon
Zest of ¼ orange and juice
of ½ orange
800g pork tenderloin
1 teaspoon sunflower oil

FOR THE CAULIFLOWER

2 tablespoons olive oil
1kg cauliflower (approx.)
1 lemon – juice of ½, the
other ½ finely chopped
2 red onions, cut in wedges
80g pickled garlic
80g black olives
Small handful of parsley,
finely chopped
Sea salt and black pepper

Preheat the oven to 200°C (180°C fan), gas mark 6. Put the seeds in a small pan and put them in the oven to toast as the oven heats up. Once they are light golden, remove from the oven. Add the ground spices, salt, thyme, sage and rosemary and grind everything together in a spice grinder or a pestle and mortar.

Gently warm the honey jar and use a hot spoon to measure the honey into a bowl. Add the lemon and orange zest and juice and the herb and spice mix and give it all a good stir.

Trim the pork of any sinew. Rub the pork all over with oil and oil a small roasting pan. Put the tenderloin in the pan and pour over the honey and spice mix. Rub it all over and put it into the oven on the top shelf. At the same time, put your largest roasting pan in to preheat for the cauliflower. The pork will need about 30 minutes in the oven; baste it from time to time.

Take the hot large roasting pan from the oven and add the olive oil, swirl about, then add the cauliflower (leaves and all), lemon pieces, red onions, pickled garlic and plenty of seasoning. Toss to coat everything with oil and return to the oven. The cauliflower will take about 30 minutes, but it's OK if it goes in about 10 minutes after the pork as the meat will benefit from resting in a warm place before serving.

About 5 minutes before the cauliflower is due to come out, add the olives to heat through.

Once the cauliflower is golden and just soft, add the lemon juice and parsley. Serve with slices of pork. It is delicious in a flatbread with some lettuce and chilli sauce.

PORK CHOPS BAKED WITH FENNEL, TOMATO AND POTATO

Pork and fennel are a classic combination, excellent in this all-in-one dish.

SERVES 4

2 tablespoons olive oil
2 heads fennel,
   fronds reserved,
   cut into sixths
320g small potatoes,
   cut into quarters
   lengthways
2 large red onions, each
   cut into eight wedges
4 large tomatoes
   – I favour plum
   tomatoes – cut in
   half lengthways
1 bay leaf
Couple of sprigs of
   thyme – lemon thyme
   is especially good here
1 tablespoon fennel
   seeds, crushed with
   the back of a spoon
½ lemon, a strip of zest
   peeled off, and juice
4 pork chops, approx.
   150–200g each,
   fat scored
Sea salt and black pepper

Preheat the oven to 220°C (200°C fan), gas mark 7. Put a roasting pan into the oven with the oil.

Meanwhile, blanch the fennel in boiling water for 4 minutes, then drain.

Once the oil is hot, add the potato wedges and toss them about to coat with oil, add some salt and pepper and place in the oven. Once the oven has reached temperature, add the remaining vegetables and herbs to the roasting pan, throw in the fennel seeds and strip of lemon zest, season well and mix everything together gently.

Season the chops generously on both sides and put them on top of the vegetables. Put into the oven for 25 minutes until the chops are brown and cooked through and the vegetables are done. Test by piercing a potato with a sharp knife: it should meet no resistance. Lift the chops out and leave to rest in a warm place for 5–7 minutes.

Add the lemon juice to the vegetables, taste for seasoning and leave them to keep warm in the cooling oven. When ready to serve, add any roughly chopped fennel fronds to the roasted vegetables.

BAKED HAM WITH CIDER AND LEEKS

A baked ham is a joyous thing and a lighter alternative to a Christmas glazed ham. I have included pasta in this recipe as the flavours are reminiscent of a carbonara, but leave the pasta out if cooking up a festive feast.

SERVES 6

3 leeks, sliced, using as
    much of the green part
    as possible
1.2kg piece boneless
    gammon
568ml bottle dry cider
250ml boiling water
2 tablespoons Dijon
    mustard
100ml double cream
227g tub sour cream
480g orecchiette pasta
300g greens, sliced into
    thick ribbons
Sea salt and black pepper

Preheat the oven to 180°C (160°C fan), gas mark 4, and put a roasting pan in to heat up.

Once hot, fill the pan with the sliced leeks – they may sizzle a little. It will seem like a huge amount, but as they cook slowly in the cider they will break down and become sweet and soft. Sit the gammon on top, add the cider and water and a good grinding of black pepper and place in the oven.

After 30 minutes, give the leeks a stir, turn the oven down to 150°C (130°C fan), gas mark 2, and cook for 1 hour, until the gammon is cooked: you can test its core temperature by inserting a skewer into the centre of the meat and counting to 20; pull it out and test the temperature on the inside of your wrist. Take care as it should be very hot. If it does not feel hot, put the gammon back in for another 20 minutes. Alternatively, if you have a meat thermometer, the core temperature should be around 68–70°C. Remove the ham from the roasting pan and leave to rest in a warm place.

Turn the oven up to 180°C (160°C fan), gas mark 4. Stir the mustard, cream and sour cream into the leeks and return to the oven for 10 minutes.

Meanwhile, cook the orecchiette in salted boiling water for 2 minutes less than suggested on the pack. Drain – reserving the pasta cooking water – and refresh in cold water. Stir the pasta into the leek and cream mixture, adding 100ml of the reserved hot water, and return to the oven for 7 minutes.

Meanwhile, steam the greens for a couple of minutes. Stir the greens into the pasta mixture and return to the oven for 5 minutes.

Check that everything is hot and taste for seasoning (this will depend on the saltiness of the gammon). I sometimes add a squeeze of lemon. Slice the gammon and serve with generous spoonfuls of pasta.

BEEF AND PRUNE POT PIE

Beef and prune is a wonderful traditional mixture. The beef shin needs a long cooking time, but it's all just bubbling away in the oven, so you can go off and then reap the tremendous rewards of unctuously soft beef.

SERVES 4

500ml stout
2 heaped tablespoons grain mustard
1kg beef shin off the bone, cut into 2cm cubes
2 tablespoons sunflower oil
2 leeks, sliced
2 celery sticks, sliced
3 sprigs of thyme
1 bay leaf
900ml boiling beef or vegetable stock
100g no-soak pitted prunes
1 heaped tablespoon cornflour
2 onions, finely sliced
Handful of parsley, roughly chopped
3–4 pickled walnuts, roughly chopped (optional)
Sea salt and black pepper

If you have time, mix the stout and mustard with several grindings of black pepper and pour over the beef the day before you want to make the pie. If you're in a hurry, half an hour will help.

To make the pastry, put the suet and flour in a bowl, strip the thyme leaves and scatter in along with some salt and pepper. Mix the flour and suet together, make a well in the centre and slowly add about 100ml of cold water – adding just enough to bind the dough together. Tip the dough onto a floured surface and knead briefly until smooth. Flatten into a disk and leave to rest in the fridge while you make the filling.

Preheat the oven to 200°C (180°C fan), gas mark 6. Put a large roasting pan in to heat up with the oil.

Lift the beef out of the stout and set aside. Put the stout into a large saucepan with the leeks, celery, thyme, bay leaf, stock and prunes and bring back to the boil, then turn the heat right down so it is just bubbling gently.

Dry the meat and then toss in the cornflour with a good pinch of salt and little pepper.

Once the roasting pan is hot, add the meat and onions in an even layer, then place in the oven for about 18 minutes, shaking halfway through, until the meat is well browned. Pour the hot liquid over the meat, stir thoroughly and cover with foil. Turn the oven down to 180°C (160°C fan), gas mark 4, and return the pan to the oven for about 1–1¼ hours until the meat is meltingly soft.

FOR THE SUET PASTRY

200g suet

400g plain flour, plus
    extra for dusting

2 sprigs of thyme

1 egg, beaten, to glaze

While the meat is braising, roll out the pastry and measure against your smallest roasting pan or a pie dish; leave the rolled-out pastry to rest for 5–10 minutes, as it sometimes shrinks a little. Cut out a pastry lid and some long strips to put around the rim of the pan or pie dish.

Once the filling is ready, turn the oven up to 200°C (180°C fan), gas mark 6. Stir the parsley into the pie filling and lift out the bay leaves and thyme stalks. You could also add a few roughly chopped pickled walnuts and a couple of tablespoons of the liquid from their jar. Spoon the filling into the small roasting pan or pie dish.

Put a pie funnel in the middle or, if you don't have one, use an upturned egg cup or some scrunched-up foil to support the centre of the pastry. Brush the rim of the pan or dish with egg and line with strips of pastry, then brush the pastry strips with egg and put the pastry lid on top and press down well. I usually go round again, pressing with the tines of a fork. If you have some excess pastry, cut out some decorations for the top of the pie. Cut a cross in the middle for the funnel to stick out.

Brush well with egg and bake for 20–30 minutes until the pastry is golden brown and crisp. Serve hot, with roasted root vegetables, or the roast celeriac with wholegrain mustard and rosemary (page 110).

BEEF CHILLI WITH CORNBREAD TOP

One of the great joys of cornbread is that you can keep it simple or make little additions, such as a few spring onions, some chopped chilli or even some sweetcorn.

SERVES 6

2 tablespoons
    sunflower oil
400g minced beef
3 onions, sliced
1 tablespoon chilli
    powder
2 teaspoons ground
    cumin
1 tablespoon cocoa
    powder
2 celery sticks, sliced
2 red peppers, deseeded
    and sliced
4 cloves garlic, crushed
2 teaspoons dried thyme
    or a few sprigs of fresh
340g tin sweetcorn
400g tin kidney beans,
    drained and rinsed
400g tin chopped
    tomatoes
Sea salt and black pepper

Preheat the oven to 220°C (200°C fan), gas mark 7. Put a roasting pan in to heat up, with 1 tablespoon of the oil.

Put the beef and onions in a bowl with the chilli, cumin, cocoa powder and salt and pepper and mix thoroughly. Once the oil is hot, put the beef mixture into the roasting pan, spreading it out so it covers the pan in a thin layer. Cook for 7 minutes until lightly browned, then stir well and give it another 7 minutes.

Meanwhile, for the cornbread, sift the flour, baking powder and bicarbonate of soda together into a bowl, then stir in the polenta, sugar, paprika, some salt and all but a small handful of the cheese. In another bowl, whisk together the eggs, milk or yoghurt, butter and oil, adding the spring onions, if using.

Once the beef has some colour, tip it into a bowl. Pour a small cup of boiling water into the pan and stir it about to lift off any tasty bits lurking on the pan, then pour this liquid in with the beef. Wipe the roasting pan dry, add the remaining tablespoon of oil, the celery and red peppers and cook for 10 minutes, shaking the pan after 5 minutes to make sure everything is cooking evenly.

Add the garlic, thyme, sweetcorn and beans and give everything a good stir. Return to the oven for about 7 minutes, then mix in the tomatoes and the beef, taste for seasoning and return to the oven for 10 minutes while you prepare the top.

FOR THE CORNBREAD

80g plain flour

2½ teaspoons baking
   powder

1 teaspoon bicarbonate
   of soda

300g fine polenta

1 heaped tablespoon
   soft light brown sugar

1 generous teaspoon
   smoked paprika

100g mature Cheddar,
   grated

4 eggs

240ml milk or
   plain yoghurt

30g butter, melted

90ml sunflower oil

4 spring onions, finely
   sliced (optional)

To finish the cornbread, add the wet ingredients to the dry and stir until just combined, taking care not to overmix. Pour the batter over the beef chilli and scatter the remaining cheese on top. Cook for 25–35 minutes or until a thin knife blade or skewer inserted into the centre comes out clean. Serve with sour cream if you like, and perhaps a green salad.

TIP You can use this recipe to make a loaf of cornbread, which is a great accompaniment to a pan of roasted vegetables. Half the quantities would make a 450g loaf and you would need to use approximately 60ml more milk or plain yoghurt. Since it has a low flour content you can make it gluten free pretty easily by using gluten-free plain flour.

SPICE-RUBBED STEAK WITH SWEET RED ONIONS AND CROUTONS

This recipe works well with any kind of steak, the rub has a tenderising effect even if you cook the meat straight away. Leave the rub overnight or just for the time it takes to cook the onions and preheat the grill.

SERVES 4

1 tablespoon light
brown sugar

2 teaspoons salt

1 teaspoon ground
allspice

1 generous teaspoon
ground coriander

1½ teaspoons
mustard powder

4 steaks

2½ tablespoons olive oil

4 red onions, peeled
and finely sliced

Few sprigs of thyme

200ml cider or apple
juice

1 tablespoon cider
vinegar

225g rustic bread,
brown or white, cut
into 1cm chunks and
tossed in 1 tablespoon
olive oil

1 tablespoon extra
virgin olive oil

60g rocket

Make a dry rub by mixing together the sugar, salt, allspice, coriander and mustard powder. Rub it thoroughly into the beef and set aside.

Preheat the oven to 190°C (170°C fan), gas mark 5. Preheat a roasting pan with 2 tablespoons of the olive oil. Once the oil in the roasting pan is hot, add the red onions, thyme cider and cider vinegar, stir everything about thoroughly, cover with foil and return to the oven for 15 minutes for them to steam and become soft.

Once the onions are in the oven, preheat the grill to its highest setting and give it 10 minutes to be red hot.

When the onions have softened, turn the oven up to 220°C (200°C fan), gas mark 7, and remove the foil. Lift out the onions and all but a tablespoon of the liquid in the roasting pan. Add the chunks of bread to the roasting pan and toss everything together well. Return to the hotter oven to let any remaining cooking liquor evaporate and the bread become golden and crisp, this will take about 8–10 minutes and it is worth shaking everything about after a few minutes. Once they look ready, take out and set aside.

Once you have returned the croutons to the hotter oven. Oil a roasting pan which will fit under the grill and place the steaks on it, turn them over a couple of times so both sides get oiled. Place the steaks under the grill for about 4 minutes on each side for rare or add on a couple more minutes per side for more cooked steak. Set the meat aside to rest in a warm place for 5 minutes.

Toss the croutons, warm red onions and their cooking liquor with the rocket, extra virgin olive oil and a dose of seasoning. Top with the sliced steak.

EASY MOUSSAKA

Moussaka has such fabulous flavours, but it can be quite a process. You will need two pans for this simple version, which has a quick and easy topping of Greek yoghurt, feta, mint and eggs.

SERVES 4

3 tablespoons
sunflower oil
500g minced lamb
2 onions, finely sliced
2 teaspoons ground
cinnamon
2 teaspoons paprika
2 small aubergines,
sliced 1–2cm thick
2 large cloves garlic,
crushed or finely
grated
1 bay leaf
2 generous sprigs
of dill, chopped
400g tin chopped
tomatoes
250ml boiling lamb
or vegetable stock
Sea salt and black pepper

Preheat the oven to 220°C (200°C fan), gas mark 7. Put a roasting pan in to heat up with 1½ tablespoons of the oil.

Mix the lamb and onions with the spices and plenty of salt and pepper. Place in the hot roasting pan and brown in the oven for 15 minutes, stirring occasionally to break up the meat, until the onions are starting to soften.

Meanwhile, toss the aubergine slices with the remaining oil and a generous pinch of salt. Place the slices in one layer in a second roasting pan and put in the oven to soften and brown – this should take about 10–15 minutes – turning the slices over halfway through. Set the aubergines aside.

Turn the oven down to 200°C (180°C fan), gas mark 6, and add the garlic, bay leaf, dill, tomatoes and hot stock to the lamb mix, stir thoroughly and return to the oven for 15 minutes, stirring from time to time. If the mixture is looking dry add a cup of boiling water.

FOR THE TOPPING

2 eggs

400g Greek yoghurt

200g feta, crumbled

Small handful of
  coriander

Couple of sprigs of mint,
  thick stalks removed

25g pine nuts

While the lamb is cooking, make the topping. In a food processor or using a stick blender, blend together all the ingredients except for the pine nuts. Season to taste.

Taste the lamb mixture for seasoning then lay the aubergine slices over the lamb. Pour the topping over and scatter over the pine nuts. Return to the oven for 20 minutes until the topping is set and golden brown. Serve with a green salad.

DAWN'S SLOW-COOKED SHOULDER OF LAMB WITH CHINESE PANCAKES

This comes from my friend's mum and is an absolute winner. It is super simple and all you need is time while it cooks – time when you can be doing other things. It's a great hands-on meal to enjoy with friends.

SERVES 6

1kg piece lamb
    shoulder, boned
6cm thumb of ginger,
    wiped clean and
    finely grated
4 heaped teaspoons
    five spice powder
3 tablespoons rice
    wine vinegar
3 tablespoons soy sauce
3 tablespoons honey
Sea salt and black pepper

TO SERVE

24 Chinese pancakes
    or soft flatbreads
200g jar hoisin sauce
1 cucumber, sliced into
    long thin sticks
8 spring onions,
    cut in half and
    sliced lengthways
    into quarters

Preheat the oven to 220°C (200°C fan), gas mark 7.

To cook the lamb, mix together all the ingredients except 1 tablespoon of honey. Season the lamb with salt and rub the mixture all over. Wrap in two layers of foil, place in a roasting pan and cook for 20 minutes.

Turn the oven down to 180°C (160°C fan), gas mark 4, and cook for 3 hours, by which time the meat should be meltingly soft.

Open up the foil, drizzle over the last spoonful of honey and return to the oven with the foil open. Leave for about 10–15 minutes for the honey glaze to crisp up the skin. Remove from the oven and leave to rest in a warm place for 15 minutes.

Meanwhile, assemble all the accompaniments and wrap the pancakes in foil.

When the lamb has rested, lift it out of the roasting pan and pour any juices that are sitting in the foil into the pan and return it to the oven to heat through. Put the pancakes in the oven at the same time.

Break the lamb up into bite-sized pieces: it will naturally shred, having been cooked for so long. Put it into a serving dish and pour over the cooking juices from the oven.

Everyone has their own way of eating this, but I go for a good smear of hoisin sauce on the pancake, followed by cucumber, spring onions and meat before rolling up the pancake.

LAMB CHOPS WITH SPICED ROOTS AND TAHINI AND ROAST GARLIC SAUCE

Ras el hanout is a spice blend found in North Africa. The name in Arabic means 'head of the shop' and implies a mixture of the best spices the seller has to offer. These days it's readily available from supermarkets.

SERVES 4

8 lamb chops

4 potatoes, scrubbed,
   not peeled, cut into
   3cm chunks

4 large carrots, cut
   into 3cm lengths

1 small swede,
   peeled and cut
   into 2cm chunks

2 small red onions, cut
   in half and half again

4 spring onions

8 fat cloves garlic, any
   loose skin removed

1–2 tablespoons
   sunflower oil
   (optional)

Preheat the oven to 180°C (160°C fan), gas mark 4.

Preheat the grill to its highest setting and give it 10 minutes to get really hot. Put a roasting pan under the grill to heat up. Season the lamb chops well on both sides and pop them on the hot roasting pan: they should sizzle. Grill for a couple of minutes, as close to the heat as possible, until they are browned and have rendered some fat. The underside should have browned when it hit the hot pan but if not, turn over and grill for 1–2 minutes on the other side. Remove the chops from the roasting pan and set aside.

Put the potatoes, carrots, swede, both types of onion and the garlic into the roasting pan with the lamb fat, stir to coat everything with the fat and, if there isn't enough fat, add 1–2 tablespoons of sunflower oil. Now add the ras el hanout and a good pinch of salt, stir well and place in the oven for 20 minutes.

Add the sweet potato and give everything a good stir. Return to the oven for 15 minutes.

1 generous tablespoon
   ras el hanout
1 sweet potato,
   peeled, cut in half
   lengthways and cut
   into 2cm chunks
200g cavolo nero or
   other greens, washed,
   thick stalks removed,
   thoroughly dried
1 tablespoon olive oil
Sea salt and black pepper

FOR THE SAUCE
Small handful of parsley
Few sprigs of mint, thick
   stalks removed
2 tablespoons tahini
1 tablespoon sesame
   seeds
75ml hot water

Meanwhile, make the sauce: put all the ingredients in a food processor or blender and whizz until smooth and the consistency of double cream. Add more hot water if necessary. Leave the sauce in the machine.

Put the cavolo nero in a bowl with the olive oil and some salt and toss together while roughly tearing up the leaves.

Check on the roots in the oven: they should be crisp around the edges and nearly cooked. Add the cavolo nero and cook for 10 minutes more. Remove the roasting pan from the oven, fish out the garlic cloves and set aside: it sounds like a needle in a haystack task, but it isn't that difficult. Put the lamb chops on top of the vegetables and return to the oven for 7 minutes to heat the chops through.

Now squeeze the garlic cloves out of their skins, add to the tahini sauce and whizz again. Season with salt to taste.

Once the chops are hot, leave them to rest in a warm place for 5 minutes. Leave the vegetables in the cooling oven and put in some plates to warm. Serve the chops on a pile of the spiced roots with a spoonful of sauce over the top.

LAMB STEAKS IN MOJO VERDE WITH ROAST POTATOES AND GREEN PEPPER

Mojo verde is an excellent sauce from the Canary Islands, its main components being fresh coriander, cumin, garlic and chilli – but not enough chilli to make it fiery. You will need two pans.

SERVES 2

2 large potatoes, scrubbed, not peeled, sliced to the thickness of a pound coin
1 large green pepper, deseeded and cut into 2cm wide strips
1 onion, sliced into 1cm circles
2 tablespoons olive oil
2 lamb leg steaks
Sea salt and black pepper

FOR THE MOJO VERDE
1 large clove garlic, sliced
3 tablespoons sherry vinegar
Large handful of coriander, chopped, including the stalks
1 green chilli, deseeded if you prefer, sliced
1½ teaspoons ground cumin, toasted
1 teaspoon sea salt
10 tablespoons extra virgin olive oil

Preheat the oven to 200°C (180°C fan), gas mark 6.

Toss the potatoes, pepper and onion with the olive oil and a good pinch of salt and pepper in a roasting pan. Bake for 30 minutes until everything is golden and soft, shaking the pan halfway through to make sure that nothing is sticking.

Meanwhile, season the leg steaks well with salt and make the mojo. Put the garlic, sherry vinegar, coriander, chilli, cumin and salt in a food processor and whizz to a paste. Slowly add the olive oil with the motor running until you have a smooth sauce. Spoon a generous amount of the sauce over the lamb steaks. Set the rest of the mojo aside.

Once the vegetables are soft, turn the oven right down and leave them in to keep warm.

Preheat the grill to its highest setting and give it 5–7 minutes to heat up. Grill the lamb, close to the heat, for about 4 minutes until brown. Turn over and cook for 4 minutes on the other side. Leave to rest for 5 minutes.

Serve the lamb with a pile of the potatoes and extra mojo sauce.

TIP Mojo verde keeps well in a jar in the fridge and has so many uses – it can be stirred through rice or pasta, rubbed onto fish or even spread over toast.

FISH

FISH BAKED WITH TOMATO SAUCE AND GNOCCHI

Making tomato sauce in the oven is a revelation – it becomes such a simple task and is much less likely to stick. I keep a supply in my freezer to use with pasta or on a pizza base.

SERVES 4

1–2 tablespoons olive oil
500g gnocchi
4 x 130g firm white
  fish fillets
Sea salt and black pepper
½ lemon, cut into
  wedges, to serve

FOR THE TOMATO SAUCE

2 tablespoons olive oil
30g butter
3 red onions, finely sliced
4 cloves garlic, sliced
1 large red chilli,
  deseeded and chopped
1 tablespoon sherry
  vinegar
400g tin chopped
  tomatoes
250ml boiling water or
  fish or vegetable stock
1 bay leaf
2 sprigs of thyme
½–1 teaspoon sugar
1 tablespoon capers
Small bunch of basil,
  chopped (optional)

Preheat the oven to 180°C (160°C fan), gas mark 4. Start by making the tomato sauce. Put a roasting pan in to heat up with the olive oil and the butter. When the butter has melted, add the onions, stir and add a good pinch of salt. Return to the oven for 15 minutes, stirring every now and then, until soft and sweet and very lightly golden brown. Add the garlic and chilli and return to the oven for a couple of minutes.

Turn the oven up to 200°C (180°C fan), gas mark 6. Splash in the sherry vinegar and return the pan to the oven for a minute or two, for the vinegar to evaporate. Add the tomatoes, hot water or stock, bay leaf, thyme, ½ teaspoon salt and the sugar, and bake for 30 minutes, stirring halfway through, until the sauce has reduced slightly.

Fish out the bay leaf and thyme, tip the sauce into a food processor and blend until smooth, adding a little more hot water if the sauce seems very thick. Stir in the capers and basil, if using.

Rinse and dry the roasting pan, then oil the base of the pan. Scatter over the gnocchi in an even layer, then cover with the tomato sauce. Bake for about 10 minutes to start the gnocchi heating through.

Season the fish fillets well on both sides. Place them on top of the gnocchi, skin-side up, and drizzle over the remaining olive oil. Bake for about 10–15 minutes until the fish is cooked: the skin should be crisp and will lift off easily when the fish is ready. Serve with small lemon wedges to squeeze over.

TIP Once accustomed to the tomato sauce in the oven method, you can add and subtract ingredients at will. Jarred peppers or olives to chase away winter blues or fresh herbs to complement whatever else you are cooking.

SMOKED HADDOCK, BROCCOLI AND FARFALLE

With this recipe I had in mind an interpretation of macaroni and/or cauliflower cheese.
The result is a lot lighter, with the added bonus of smoked fish.

SERVES 4

2 tablespoons olive oil
200g farfalle
250g broccoli, broken
  into small florets
2 cloves garlic, crushed
  or finely grated
Generous pinch of
  chilli flakes
320g undyed smoked
  haddock, skinned
Juice of ½ lemon
40g Parmesan, grated

Preheat the oven to 180°C (160°C fan), gas mark 4. Put a roasting pan in to heat up with the olive oil.

Meanwhile, cook the farfalle in boiling salted water for 10 minutes and steam the broccoli until very tender – I steam the broccoli over the pasta.

Once the oil is hot, add the garlic and chilli flakes and stir for a couple of minutes, then add the smoked haddock. When the pasta is ready, drain it, reserving the water. Pour 400ml of pasta water over the fish and place in the oven for 10 minutes until it is just cooked. Using a slotted spoon, lift out the fish and set aside.

Add the broccoli to the roasting pan and start to break it up with a spoon, then place in the oven for about 15 minutes, stirring halfway through, until it is really soft.

When the haddock has cooled slightly, flake it into nice big pieces, add to the pasta and toss with the lemon juice.

When the broccoli has broken down and the liquid reduced, add the pasta and fish and the Parmesan. Return to the oven for 5 minutes to heat through. Serve immediately, with extra Parmesan or lemon if you like.

A little tomato salad would go really nicely with this.

BAKED MUSSELS WITH TOMATO AND FREGOLA

This is a wonderfully messy dish that requires hands-on eating! It's great fun, but make sure you provide lots of napkins and a bowl for the shells, and bread for mopping up the sauce. You will need two pans.

SERVES 4

3 tablespoons olive oil

6 banana shallots, cut in half lengthways and sliced

20g butter

1 large leek, cut in half lengthways and sliced

1 large head fennel, cut into quarters and sliced (fronds reserved)

3 cloves garlic, crushed or finely grated

1–2 teaspoons chilli flakes (to taste)

1 teaspoon fennel seeds, crushed or chopped

250g fregola or giant couscous

125ml white wine or cider (optional)

400ml boiling fish or vegetable stock

300g passata

1kg mussels, scrubbed, beards removed, rinsed

3 sprigs of mint, leaves chopped

Juice of 1 lemon

Sea salt

Preheat the oven to 180°C (160°C fan), gas mark 4. Put the smaller of your two roasting pans in to heat up, with 2 tablespoons of the olive oil.

Once the oven is hot, add the shallots, butter and a generous pinch of salt to the roasting pan and place in the oven for 10 minutes.

Stir in the leek and fennel and return to the oven for 10 minutes until the vegetables are starting to soften. Add the garlic, chilli and fennel seeds and cook for another 5 minutes.

Add the fregola and stir well. Now add the wine or cider, if using (if not, add an extra 125ml stock or water), the stock and passata and return to the oven for 10 minutes.

Turn the oven up to 220°C (200°C fan), gas mark 7. Give everything a good stir and if the fregola mix is looking very thick you can add more hot water – about 150ml. Return this roasting pan to the oven and place a larger roasting pan, with the remaining tablespoon of olive oil, in to get good and hot. Have your mussels ready in a colander.

When the oven is hot, take out the large roasting pan and throw in the mussels, they should sizzle a little. Add the tomato mixture and give everything a good stir, adding some more hot water or stock if it seems thick. Return to the oven until the mussels open – this will take about 10–15 minutes. When all the mussels are open, stir in the mint and lemon juice, garnish with the reserved fennel leaves, and serve immediately.

YOGHURT-BAKED FISH WITH CHILLI SWEET POTATO AND PEANUT CHUTNEY

Harissa is a North African spice paste made with cumin, chilli and oil
— when mixed with yoghurt it will give the fish a bit of spice without being too fiery.

SERVES 2

2 x 130g skinless firm
   white fish fillets
100g natural yoghurt
1 tablespoon harissa
Sea salt

FOR THE SWEET POTATO

1 large sweet potato,
   unpeeled, cut into
   wedges lengthways
1½ tablespoons olive oil
1 teaspoon chilli powder
1 teaspoon cumin seeds
1 large clove garlic,
   crushed or finely grated

FOR THE PEANUT CHUTNEY

40g raw peanuts
2 teaspoons garam masala
Small handful coriander
Juice of 1 lime
1 tablespoon dark
   brown sugar
1 green chilli, deseeded
   and roughly chopped
1 small red onion,
   chopped

Preheat the oven 200°C (180°C fan), gas mark 6. For the peanut chutney, put the peanuts in a roasting pan with 1 teaspoon of salt and garam masala and put them in the oven to toast as the oven heats up. When lightly browned, set aside.

Place the fish in a dish. Mix the yoghurt, harissa and a generous pinch of salt together – taste and add more harissa if you like it spicy. Pour the yoghurt mixture over the fish, gently rubbing it in, and leave to marinate while you prepare the sweet potato.

Put the sweet potato wedges in the roasting pan, add the olive oil and toss together very well. Add the remaining ingredients, season with salt, mix thoroughly and bake for 15 minutes.

Give the sweet potatoes a good shake and add the fish to the roasting pan: either push the potatoes to the sides of the pan and put the fish in the middle, or put the fish on top of the potatoes. Return to the oven for 15 minutes until the fish is cooked.

Meanwhile, make the chutney. Put the spiced peanuts into a food processor (reserve some to garnish at the end) with the coriander, lime juice, sugar, chilli and onion and whizz everything together to a smooth paste.

When the fish is done, sprinkle with the reserved roasted peanuts and serve hot with a dollop of peanut chutney. This is nice served with naan bread or rice.

RICE BAKED WITH CRAB, PEAS AND BROCCOLI

I am a big fan of purple and white sprouting broccoli and, when they are in season in early spring, I use them instead of regular broccoli – in April/May I will use asparagus. If you can't get crab, brown shrimps are also lovely.

SERVES 4

50g butter

3 tablespoons olive oil

5 banana shallots, finely sliced

360g arborio or other short grain rice

100ml white wine or cider (optional)

900ml boiling vegetable or fish stock

120g frozen peas, defrosted

100g broccoli, broken into bite-sized florets

150g crab meat (brown, white or a mixture)

Small handful of dill, finely chopped

3 sprigs of tarragon, leaves finely chopped

Small handful of parsley, finely chopped

Grated zest and juice of 1 lemon

Sea salt

Preheat the oven to 180°C (160°C fan), gas mark 4, and put a roasting pan in to heat up.

Once hot, add the butter, olive oil, shallots and a good pinch of salt and return to the oven for 5 minutes. Give the shallots a stir and cook for another 5 minutes until softened: if they are looking a bit brown, cover with foil.

Once the shallots are soft, stir in the rice to coat well with the buttery mixture. If you like, add the wine or cider and return the pan to the oven for 5 minutes until the wine is absorbed. Add the hot stock (adding an extra 100ml if you didn't use wine or cider), stir, then cook for 20 minutes.

Add the peas and broccoli, stir well, and return to the oven for 5 minutes.

Stir in the crab and cook for another 5 minutes. By this time the stock will have been absorbed and the rice should be cooked through but the dish shouldn't be entirely dry.

Mix the herbs with the lemon zest. Set aside a tablespoon of the mixture.

Stir the herb mixture and lemon juice into the rice, cover the roasting pan with a clean tea towel and leave to settle for a few minutes. I usually put the plates in the cooling oven to warm up.

Serve the rice with a little of the reserved herb mixture scattered over the top.

TUNA AND POTATO BAKED OMELETTE

This thick Spanish-style omelette is quick and easy to make. It is also really good cold. The Spanish often eat a slice of tortilla in a soft roll with a smear of mayo and some salad for a delicious picnic lunch.

SERVES 4

2 large potatoes, cut
    into 2cm chunks
1 large red onion, sliced
4½ tablespoons olive oil
5 eggs
160g tuna in spring
    water, drained and
    flaked
80g frozen peas,
    defrosted
Small handful of
    parsley, chopped
Sea salt and black pepper

Preheat the oven to 180°C (160°C fan), gas mark 4.

Put the potato chunks and onion in a roasting pan with 3 tablespoons of the olive oil and a good pinch of salt. Place in the oven for 15–20 minutes until soft and a little brown at the edges.

Break the eggs into a jug or bowl, season well, add a dash of olive oil and whisk thoroughly. Add the tuna, peas and parsley and more seasoning.

Tip the potato and onion mixture into a bowl.

Rinse out the roasting pan and dry well. Add the remaining tablespoon of olive oil to the pan and place in the oven for 5 minutes to heat the oil.

Take the roasting pan out of the oven and add the egg mixture and then spoon the potatoes evenly throughout the egg. Shake the pan gently then return to the oven until set, which will take about 25 minutes. The middle sets last, so check that it's done.

Remove from the oven and let the omelette sit for a few minutes. Run a knife around the edge and turn it out onto a board – or serve it straight from the pan. Serve with aïoli or herby mayonnaise and a salad; in the summer I would always go with a tomato salad.

SALMON BAKED WITH HORSERADISH AND HOT POTATO AND BEETROOT SALAD

This dish has vibrant colours and well-matched flavours. The idea is to cook two pieces of salmon with a horseradish mixture sandwiched between them. You need two roasting pans: one for the fish and one for potatoes.

SERVES 4

2 x 300g pieces of salmon
   fillet, skinned
2 tablespoons grated
   horseradish
60g crème fraîche
Grated zest and juice
   of ½ lemon
Small bunch of chives,
   snipped
Generous drizzle of
   sunflower oil
Sea salt and black pepper

**FOR THE POTATO AND
BEETROOT SALAD**

300g new potatoes,
   cut into quarters
2 tablespoons olive oil
200g cooked beetroot,
   cut into 3cm chunks
Small bunch of dill,
   chopped
3 spring onions, sliced
1 tablespoon balsamic
   vinegar
20g salad leaves
   or pea shoots

Preheat the oven 180°C (160°C fan), gas mark 4. Put the potatoes in a large roasting pan and drizzle over a generous tablespoon of olive oil and plenty of seasoning. Roast for 20 minutes.

Meanwhile, for the salmon, mix together the horseradish, crème fraîche, lemon zest, chives and plenty of seasoning. Place a piece of foil large enough to wrap the salmon in a roasting pan. Oil the foil with the sunflower oil and place one fillet on it, skinned-side down. Season the fish and spread over the horseradish filling. Season the other piece of fish and place on top of the filling with the skinned side facing up. Season, then squeeze over the lemon and add about 4 tablespoons of water. Bring the foil together to seal the parcel. Place in the oven for about 20 minutes.

While the oven is open, shake the pan of potatoes; they will need another 20 minutes. Add the beetroot after 10 minutes.

After 20 minutes, check the salmon. Take the pan out of the oven and very carefully open the foil. Insert a knife blade into the centre of the fish: the flesh should look opaque, and will be falling into flakes. If it is a little on the translucent side, that is fine, as it will continue to cook in its warm parcel while you finish the potato and beetroot salad. If you are at all concerned, return the salmon to the oven for another 5 minutes.

When the potatoes are cooked, take them out of the oven and add the dill and spring onions and taste for seasoning. Toss in the remaining olive oil and the balsamic. Once mixed, gently fold the salad leaves through.

Lift the salmon from its parcel and cut into four slices. Pour over any pan juices and serve immediately with the hot potato and beetroot salad.

GREEN COUSCOUS WITH PRAWNS

A brilliant green colour and easily adaptable. Make a vegetarian version of this dish by replacing the prawns with crumbled feta, and use vegetarian stuffed olives.

SERVES 4

300g couscous
500ml boiling vegetable
  or fish stock
200g frozen peas,
  defrosted
150g frozen spinach,
  defrosted
40g butter
300g North Atlantic
  peeled prawns
4 spring onions,
  thickly sliced
90g green olives stuffed
  with anchovies,
  roughly chopped
30g preserved lemon,
  shredded small, or
  grated zest of 1 lemon
Juice of 1 lemon
Small handful of parsley,
  roughly chopped
Sea salt and black pepper

Put the couscous in a bowl and pour over 350ml of the hot stock, cover and leave to expand for a good 10 minutes.

Preheat the oven to 180°C (160°C fan), gas mark 4.

Put the peas, spinach and butter into a blender or food processor with the rest of the hot stock and whizz to a coarse purée.

Once the couscous has absorbed all the stock, stir it well with a fork or rub between finger and thumb to get rid of any clumps. Stir in the vibrant green purée and tip the couscous into a roasting pan with the prawns, spring onions, olives, preserved lemon or lemon zest and plenty of seasoning. Place in the oven to heat through for 15–20 minutes.

Once the couscous is hot, stir in the lemon juice, taste for seasoning and add the parsley. Serve in warmed bowls.

SPICED WHITE FISH WITH NOODLES AND BROTH

Making noodle soup in the oven is just as easy as doing it on the hob. You will need two roasting pans, one for the broth and one for the fish. You can coat the fish in the spice mix several hours in advance if you like.

SERVES 2

2 x 130g skinless firm
white fish steaks, such
as monkfish
1 teaspoon soft light
brown sugar
1 teaspoon sea salt
1 teaspoon ground ginger
1 teaspoon ground
coriander
½ teaspoon cayenne
pepper
Grated zest and juice
of ½ lime
1 tablespoon sunflower oil
300ml boiling fish stock
3cm thumb of ginger,
peeled and grated
2 cloves garlic, crushed
or finely grated
2 spring onions, sliced
diagonally into long
thin pieces
1 large carrot, cut
into matchsticks
1 celery stick, sliced
100g fresh thick
udon noodles
Handful of coriander,
roughly chopped

Place the fish in a dish. Mix the sugar, salt, spices and lime zest together in a small bowl. Brush the fish with oil on both sides then rub the spice mixture all over. Set aside in the fridge for up to 5 hours if you have the time, but even 15 minutes while the oven is heating will be beneficial.

Preheat the oven to 200°C (180°C fan), gas mark 6.

Pour the hot fish stock into a deep roasting pan, add the ginger and garlic and put into the oven for 5 minutes.

Lightly oil a small roasting pan, add the fish and put into the oven – it should take about 10 minutes to cook.

At the same time, add the spring onions, carrot and celery to the broth in the oven.

Cook the noodles as directed on the pack, then add to the fish broth. Taste and add salt if needed.

When the fish is ready, squeeze the lime juice over it.

Add the coriander to the broth. Ladle the noodles and broth into serving bowls and put a piece of fish on top. Pour over any juices from the fish roasting pan and serve immediately with some coriander leaves to garnish.

ROAST MACKEREL AND SPRING ONIONS WITH TARRAGON

Roasting small whole fish is a super simple quick supper.
The herby sauce has enough acidity to cut the richness of the mackerel.

SERVES 2

2 whole mackerel, gutted
1 lemon – ½ thinly
   sliced, the other ½ cut
   in half to serve
Small handful of herbs
   (parsley, tarragon, etc)
2 tablespoons olive oil
6 spring onions, trimmed
   and left whole
Sea salt and black pepper

FOR THE SAUCE

100g stale bread
2 tablespoons white
   wine vinegar
Small handful of flat-leaf
   parsley, chopped
5 sprigs of tarragon,
   leaves removed – use
   the stalks to go in the
   fish cavities
1 egg, hard-boiled –
   white finely chopped,
   yolk crumbled
6 tablespoons extra
   virgin olive oil
1 banana shallot, diced
1 heaped tablespoon
   capers

Start by making the sauce. Soak the bread in water until it is soft but not disintegrating. Lift it out of the water and give it a good squeeze, then put the bread, vinegar, herbs and boiled egg yolk in a food processor and whizz to a smooth paste, gradually adding the oil: you don't want the bread whizzing round for too long or it might go gluey. Once all the oil is incorporated, turn the sauce into a bowl and add the egg white, shallot and capers. Taste for seasoning.

Preheat the oven to 200°C (180°C fan), gas mark 6.

Cut a couple of slashes on each side of the fish and stuff the cavities with lemon slices, herbs and seasoning. Season the outsides too.

Oil a roasting pan and add the spring onions in a row, season, drizzle with more oil and place the fish on top. Drizzle the remaining oil over the fish.

When the oven is hot, roast the mackerel for 12–15 minutes until they are cooked through: the skin will peel off easily if the fish is done. Serve the fish and spring onions with a good dollop of the sauce and a wedge of lemon.

FANCY FISH FINGERS AND BEANS

Fish fingers are universally popular. A polenta coating gives them an extra crispness, but dried breadcrumbs such as panko work just as well. You can use any white fish, but if using flat fish fillets they will need a shorter cooking time than suggested here. The beans are cooked separately and make a good vegan side dish or light supper.

SERVES 4

1 egg
100g fine polenta
4 x 120g skinless white
　fish fillets, cut into
　3cm wide pieces
4 tablespoons olive oil
Sea salt and black pepper
½ lemon, cut into wedges
　to serve

FOR THE BEANS

3 tablespoons olive oil
1 red onion, thinly sliced
2 celery sticks, finely
　sliced
2 cloves garlic, crushed
　or finely grated
1 tablespoon sherry
　vinegar
400g tin borlotti beans,
　drained and rinsed
400g tin cherry tomatoes
400ml boiling vegetable
　stock
Few sprigs of dill,
　chopped (optional)

Preheat the oven to 180°C (160°C fan), gas mark 4. Put a small roasting pan in to heat up with 2 tablespoons of the olive oil for the beans.

Once hot, add the onion and a good pinch of salt and place in the oven to soften for about 7 minutes. Add the remaining tablespoon of oil and the celery, mix thoroughly and return to the oven for another 7 minutes until it has all started to soften and get some gentle golden colour. Add the garlic and vinegar to the onions and celery, give it all a good stir and pop back in the oven for a couple of minutes.

Turn the oven up to 200°C (180°C fan), gas mark 6. Add the beans, cherry tomatoes and vegetable stock to the roasting pan, stir and return to the oven for 20 minutes until the liquid has reduced down to a sauce.

While the beans are cooking, make the fish fingers. In a shallow dish, whisk the egg with 2–3 tablespoons of water and some salt and pepper. Put the polenta in another shallow dish. Line a pan with a reusable silicone baking mat or foil. Dip the fish pieces into the polenta and then into the egg; once coated with egg, let any excess drip off before putting them back into the polenta. Ensure each piece is evenly coated with polenta before placing in a single layer on the baking mat or foil.

Preheat a large roasting pan, adding the 4 tablespoons of olive oil. Once this oil is smoking hot, add the fish fingers in a single layer and cook for about 5 minutes until crisp and golden, then turn over and cook for another 5 minutes – if you have used flat fish fillets they will need much less time. Lift the fish onto FSC kitchen paper to absorb any excess oil.

By the time the fish is cooked the beans should be ready too. Taste and adjust the seasoning and add the dill. Serve immediately, with lemon wedges to squeeze over the fish.

PLAICE BAKED WITH FENNEL, POTATOES AND CIDER

*Flat fish are really quick to cook and convenient if you can get them ready filleted.
Plaice vary in size, but the important thing is that the fish should be really fresh.*

SERVES 2

2 tablespoons olive oil
6 new potatoes, scrubbed
   and cut in half
   lengthways
1 large head fennel,
   trimmed and
   finely sliced
2 red onions, sliced
1 red apple, skin on,
   cored and cut into
   eight wedges
120ml cider
Few sprigs of parsley,
   chopped
2–4 skinless plaice fillets,
   about 300g total weight
20g butter
Sea salt and black pepper

Preheat the oven to 200°C (180°C fan), gas mark 6. Put a roasting pan in to heat up with 1½ tablespoons of the olive oil.

Once hot, add the potatoes and cook for 15 minutes.

Meanwhile, mix the fennel, onions and apple together with a good pinch of salt and set aside.

Add the cider to the roasting pan and return to the oven for 5 minutes.

Now add the fennel mixture and stir well. Test the potatoes with the point of a sharp knife: it should meet no resistance, but if necessary cook for a little longer.

Stir in the parsley and sit the fish fillets on top, skinned-side down. Season the fish and dot with the butter. Bake for 7 minutes or until the fish is opaque. Serve immediately.

FISH WRAPPED IN HAM, WITH BUTTER BEANS AND SUN-DRIED TOMATOES

This is inspired by saltimbocca, an Italian dish of veal wrapped in Parma ham. The salty ham works well with firm white fish. You will need a second roasting pan for the butter bean mixture.

SERVES 4

1 tablespoon olive oil
1 red onion, finely sliced
Grated zest and juice of
  1 lemon
2 x 400g tins butter
  beans, drained and
  rinsed
4 x 130g skinless firm
  white fish fillets
4 sage leaves, rolled up
  together and sliced
  into thin ribbons
4 slices of Parma ham
100g semi-dried or
  sun-dried tomatoes
  in oil, drained and
  chopped, plus
  2 tablespoons of
  their oil
120g baby spinach
125ml boiling water
Sea salt and black pepper
½ lemon, cut into wedges
  to serve (optional)

Preheat the oven to 200°C (180°C fan), gas mark 6. Put a large roasting pan brushed with a little of the olive oil into the oven to heat up.

Mix the red onion with the lemon juice and a good pinch of salt and leave to macerate while you prepare the fish.

Put the butter beans into a pan or bowl of boiling water to heat through.

Line up the fish fillets in a row, season well with salt and pepper, scatter over the sage and lemon zest and drizzle over the remaining olive oil, then wrap each piece of fish in a slice of ham – don't worry if it's not entirely enveloped. Put the seam of the ham on the underside of the fish. Once the roasting pan is hot, lift the fish fillets into the hot pan, seam-side down, and put in the oven.

Drain the beans and place in a smaller roasting pan. Add the tomatoes and their oil, the spinach, plenty of seasoning and the boiling water, and place in the oven at the same time as the fish.

By the time the fish is cooked – about 10 minutes – the beans should be hot and the spinach wilted. Add the pink lemony onions and all their juice to the beans. Serve the fish on top of the beans with a small lemon wedge to squeeze over if you like.

COD, ORZO, SWEET POTATO AND TAPENADE

The southern French olive paste known as tapenade is great with fish: the salty umami flavours bring all the elements of this dish together. You can get different types of tapenade, but for this dish I favour a green one.

SERVES 4

2 tablespoons olive oil
1 large sweet potato, peeled and cut into 3cm chunks
2 banana shallots, quartered lengthways
320g orzo
650ml boiling vegetable or fish stock
4 x 130g skinless cod fillets
2 tablespoons green tapenade
Small handful of basil
Sea salt and black pepper
½ lemon, cut into wedges to serve

Preheat the oven to 200°C (180°C fan), gas mark 6. Put a roasting pan in to heat up with the olive oil.

Once the oil is hot, add the sweet potato and shallots and roast for 15 minutes until the vegetables have started to soften.

Add the orzo and stir until it is well mixed with the vegetables. Add the boiling stock and return to the oven for 15 minutes.

Meanwhile, season the fish with salt and pepper and divide the tapenade between the four fillets, smoothing it over the top of each one.

By now the orzo will have absorbed most of the stock. Tear the basil into the pasta and give everything a good stir, taste and adjust the seasoning and sit the fish fillets on top. Bake for 12 minutes until the fish is opaque and readily breaks into flakes. Serve immediately, with small lemon wedges to squeeze over.

SPICED PRAWN FILO PIE

The flavours in this pie are based on those in a Moroccan pastilla – a filo pastry pie filled with pigeon, apricots and spices. This version has prawns, spinach and red peppers, which marry well with the spicing.

SERVES 4

1 tablespoon olive oil

3 red onions, sliced

2 red peppers,
deseeded and cut
into 2cm wide strips

1 tablespoon ground
cumin

1 heaped teaspoon
ground cinnamon

2 teaspoons paprika

250g frozen large
cold-water prawns,
defrosted

2 fat cloves garlic,
crushed or finely grated

250g cooked brown rice

200g frozen spinach,
defrosted and
squeezed dry

Grated zest and juice
of ½ lemon

Small handful of
coriander, chopped

80g butter, melted

250g filo pastry

2 tablespoons
sesame seeds

Sea salt

Preheat the oven to 200°C (180°C fan), gas mark 6. Put a roasting pan in to heat up with the olive oil.

Once hot, add the onions, peppers, spices and a generous pinch of salt and return to the oven for 15 minutes.

Meanwhile, mix together the prawns, garlic, rice, spinach, lemon zest and juice and coriander. Once the peppers and onions are soft, add the prawn mixture, taste and adjust the seasoning.

Butter a small (approx. 30 x 20cm) roasting pan and line with two overlapping sheets of filo pastry, leaving plenty hanging over the edge; brush the pastry with melted butter and scatter over a quarter of the sesame seeds. Repeat the process twice more, using a total of six sheets of filo, but not scattering sesame seeds over the final layer.

Add the prawn mixture and then fold all the overhanging filo over the filling – it should completely cover the filling. Brush the top with butter, scrunch up the ends and scatter over the remaining sesame seeds. Bake for 25 minutes until the pastry is crisp and golden and the filling is piping hot.

ANA'S FISH PARCELS

Ana, a great friend of mine from Spain, taught me a lot about cooking and encouraged me to experiment. This is one of her recipes. You will need two roasting pans – and string if using baking parchment for the parcels.

SERVES 2

1½ tablespoons olive oil
3 cloves garlic,
   finely sliced
1 teaspoon sweet
   smoked paprika
1 leek, finely sliced
1 potato, diced into
   small pieces
2 skinless cod loins,
   approx. 200g each
Sea salt and black pepper

**FOR THE BAKED
VEGETABLES**

1 courgette, cut into
   long thin strips using
   a peeler
1 aubergine, cut into
   long thin strips
1½ tablespoons olive oil
1 clove black garlic (or
   regular garlic), crushed
1½ tablespoons extra
   virgin olive oil
2 teaspoons balsamic
   vinegar
Couple of sprigs of
   fresh oregano, basil or
   thyme, leaves stripped
   from stalks

Preheat the oven to 180°C (160°C fan), gas mark 4. Put a large roasting pan and a small roasting pan with the olive oil into the oven to heat up.

When the oil is hot in the small pan, throw in the garlic and return to the oven until it turns light golden and crisp – don't let it burn or it will become bitter. Remove from the oven, strain off any oil into a bowl and drain the garlic on FSC kitchen paper, then toss with the paprika. Set aside: this is the garnish for the cod parcels.

Mix the leek and potato together with the garlic oil and season generously.

Cut two large rectangles of baking parchment or foil and make a bed of the leek and potato mixture in the centre of each. Season the fish and place it on the vegetables. Bring the parchment or foil up around the fish to form a parcel, leaving space for the steam to circulate. If using parchment, tie with string so it is like a spacious but well sealed bag. If using foil, fold over and crimp the top to create a nice tight seam.

Place the parcels on the hot large roasting pan and cook for about 15–20 minutes until the parcels are puffed up and full of steam.

While the fish is cooking, put the courgette and aubergine ribbons in the small roasting pan with a splash of the olive oil and season with salt and pepper. Cook for 10–15 minutes until soft and golden.

To make a dressing for the aubergine and courgette, using a stick blender, whizz together the garlic, extra virgin olive oil, balsamic and herbs until smooth. Once the vegetables are ready, toss them in the dressing.

Serve the fish in its little parcel topped with the garlic slices. Serve the courgettes and aubergines separately, to go on top of the fish once the parcel has been opened.

FISH PIE WITH A RÖSTI TOPPING

Fish pie is a firm family favourite – this one cuts out a lot of the work,
such as making a white sauce and mashed potato.

SERVES 4

500g firm white
   fish fillets
1 leek, finely sliced,
   using as much of the
   green part as possible
300ml hot milk
100g cream cheese
   with herbs and garlic
100g baby spinach
Small handful of
   parsley, chopped
Few sprigs of tarragon
   (optional), leaves
   chopped
80g smoked mackerel,
   flaked
1 tub (approx. 55g)
   potted shrimps
Grated zest and juice
   of ½ lemon
700g large red-skinned
   potatoes, peeled
2 tablespoons capers
60g butter, melted
Sea salt and black pepper

Preheat the oven to 220°C (200°C fan), gas mark 7.

Put the fish, leek and milk into a small roasting pan, season well and cover with foil. Bake for 15 minutes until the fish is cooked and the leek has softened.

Strain off the milk into a food processor and add the cream cheese, spinach and herbs. Whizz to make a smooth, thickish sauce.

Separate the fish from the leeks, remove the skin if there is any, and flake the fish. Mix together the poached fish, mackerel and leeks. Break up the potted shrimps as best you can and add them, too. Add the lemon juice and zest and stir in the herby sauce. Taste and adjust the seasoning. Spread this mixture evenly in the roasting pan.

Coarsely grate the potatoes and toss with the capers, melted butter and plenty of seasoning. Spread the potato mix evenly over the fish.

Bake for 35 minutes until the topping is golden and crisp on top and fluffy underneath. Test by piercing the potato topping with a sharp knife: it should slide through easily. Leave to stand for 5 minutes before serving. I like to have fish pie with peas.

GRILLED MUSTARD SMOKED HADDOCK AND LENTILS

I use this mustard marinade with rabbit, chicken or pork, as well as smoked fish. It's great if you can do it the night before, but is equally good if the fish only marinates for a short time before being grilled.

SERVES 4

2 spring onions, sliced

2 cloves garlic, chopped

2 tablespoons Dijon
 mustard

1 tablespoon wholegrain
 mustard

1 tablespoon cider
 vinegar

Small handful of parsley,
 roughly chopped

3 tablespoons olive oil

4 x 130g pieces of
 undyed smoked
 haddock or other
 smoked white
 fish, skinned

2 x 400g tins lentils,
 drained and rinsed

150ml boiling water

30g rocket, roughly torn

Small bunch of chives,
 snipped

Sea salt and black pepper

½ lemon, cut into wedges
 to serve (optional)

Put the spring onions, garlic, mustard, vinegar and parsley in a food processor and whizz to a smooth paste. Add 2 tablespoons of the olive oil, salt and pepper and whizz for a bit longer. Pour into a dish, add the fish and coat all over with the marinade. Cover and leave for at least 30 minutes or overnight.

If you have left it overnight, take the fish out of the fridge. Preheat the grill to its highest setting and give it 5–7 minutes to get really hot. At the same time drop the lentils into a pan of boiling water to heat them through, then drain.

Put the remaining olive oil into a roasting pan that will fit under your grill; add the lentils and some salt and pepper and stir to get them well coated with oil.

Lift the fish out of the marinade, wiping off excess marinade, and set aside on a plate.

Add the boiling water to the marinade, pour over the lentils and stir well. Place the fish on top of the lentils. Grill for about 5 minutes; if the pieces of fish are very thick, turn and grill for a few minutes on the other side until the fish is cooked and readily breaks into flakes.

Lift the fish off and set aside on a warmed plate. Stir the rocket and chives into the lentils and taste for seasoning. Spoon the lentils onto serving plates and place the fish on top. If you like, add a small lemon wedge to squeeze over.

If you want something extra, try the charred cabbage (see page 108). Or on warmer days, a bitter leaf and orange salad.

VEG

MUSHROOMS STUFFED WITH RICE, SPINACH AND PINE NUTS

*What an easy supper. A recent revelation has been ready-cooked rice and other grains in pouches
– they make all-in-one meals in the oven an absolute breeze. I have used a basmati and wild rice mix.*

SERVES 2

30g pine nuts
2 tablespoons olive oil
250g flat mushrooms,
  stalks removed –
  this should be four
  nice-sized mushrooms
250g pouch cooked
  basmati and wild rice
200g frozen spinach,
  defrosted
3 spring onions,
  finely sliced
1 large clove garlic,
  crushed or finely
  chopped
40g butter, melted
25g Parmesan-style
  vegetarian cheese,
  finely grated
15g breadcrumbs –
  fresh or panko
Sea salt and black pepper

Preheat the oven to 160°C (140°C fan), gas mark 3. Put the pine nuts in a roasting pan and put them in the oven to toast gently as the oven heats up. Their high fat content means they catch very quickly – in commercial kitchens chefs are renowned for setting three alarms and still managing to burn the pine nuts! – so watch them carefully. Once the pine nuts are golden, tip them into a bowl and set aside.

Drizzle 1 tablespoon of the olive oil into the roasting pan and add the mushrooms, white cap-side down. Drizzle the remaining oil over the mushrooms and season generously. Cook for about 15 minutes until soft.

Meanwhile, make the filling. Put the cooked rice, spinach, spring onions, garlic, butter and 20g of the cheese into the bowl with the pine nuts and stir well. Taste and adjust the seasoning.

After 15 minutes the mushrooms should be soft. Spoon the spinach mixture onto the mushrooms, then scatter over the breadcrumbs and the remaining Parmesan. Return to the oven for about 20 minutes until the stuffing is piping hot. Serve immediately.

TIP For a vegan version, replace the butter with another 3 tablespoons of olive oil and omit the cheese.

SQUASH, TOMATO AND GOATS' CHEESE STRATA

A delicious September dish, when all the wonderful squashes are appearing and the tomatoes are having their swansong – it works well with green tomatoes, too, and out of season there are tinned cherry tomatoes.

SERVES 6

2 tablespoons olive oil

500g squash, peeled, deseeded and cut into 2cm thick slices

3 red onions, cut in half and each half cut into four wedges

1 small sprig of rosemary, leaves roughly chopped

250g cherry tomatoes

125g soft goats' cheese

1–2 tablespoons chilli jam or sauce (optional)

300g sliced bread, approx. 10 medium thick slices – I like to use a white sourdough

5 eggs

200ml milk

250g crème fraîche

30g Parmesan-style vegetarian cheese, grated

Sea salt and black pepper

Preheat the oven to 180°C (160°C fan), gas mark 4. Put a roasting pan in to heat up with the olive oil.

When hot, add the squash and onions, the rosemary and plenty of seasoning. Shake everything about and place in the oven for about 15 minutes. Shake or stir well, add the cherry tomatoes and return to the oven for about 10 minutes.

Meanwhile, mix the goats' cheese with the chilli jam and spread over the bread. Cut in half diagonally to make triangles. To make the custard, whisk the eggs with the milk, crème fraîche and half of the cheese. Season well.

Once the squash has started to soften, tip the vegetables into a bowl. Using half of the bread triangles, arrange them in a layer in the roasting pan, cheese-side up, overlapping them if need be. Add the squash mixture, seasoning to taste. Then add the final layer of bread, cheese-side down.

Pour over the custard and leave to stand for at least 20 minutes or overnight in the fridge. Be sure to take it out of the fridge a good 25 minutes before you plan to cook it.

Turn the oven down to 160°C (140°C fan), gas mark 3. Scatter over the remaining Parmesan-style cheese and bake for 25–30 minutes until just set. Leave to stand for 5–7 minutes before serving. I like to serve this with a green salad.

RED PEPPERS STUFFED WITH SPICED CHICKPEAS AND AUBERGINE

When peppers and tomatoes are abundant in summer this is a great dish to serve as a vegan main course or alongside barbecued meat or fish or as part of a mezze. It's good at room temperature or straight from the oven.

SERVES 4

VEGAN

1 large aubergine, cut into 2cm cubes

2 red onions, roughly sliced

3 tablespoons olive oil

2 teaspoons ground coriander

1 teaspoon ground cumin

1 teaspoon turmeric

Pinch of chilli flakes

400g tin chickpeas, drained

4 red peppers, cut in half lengthways, deseeded and white pith removed

6 ripe tomatoes

3 cloves garlic, crushed or finely grated

3cm thumb of ginger, peeled and finely grated

Juice of ½ lemon

Generous handful of coriander, roughly chopped

Sea salt and black pepper

Coconut yoghurt, to serve

Preheat the oven to 190°C (170°C fan), gas mark 5, and put a roasting pan in to heat up.

Toss the aubergine and onions together with 1½ tablespoons of olive oil and plenty of seasoning. Once the oven is hot, add a splash of oil to the pan and swirl around. Add the aubergine and onions and shake to distribute them evenly. Roast for 15 minutes until the aubergine is golden and the onion has softened.

Sprinkle over the dry spices and return to the oven for a minute to let them toast. Add the chickpeas and then tip the mixture into a bowl, scraping with a spatula to ensure all the toasted spices come too, and set aside.

Turn the oven down to 180°C (160°C fan), gas mark 4. Place the peppers cavity-side down in the roasting pan, drizzle with olive oil and season well. Put in the oven for 10–20 minutes until softened but not cooked through.

Meanwhile, prepare the tomato sauce. Put the tomatoes, garlic and ginger in a blender and whizz until smooth.

Once the peppers have softened, remove them from the pan and set aside. Pour the tomato sauce into the hot pan. Turn the oven up to 220°C (200°C fan), gas mark 7. Return the pan to the oven to heat the sauce for about 5 minutes. Add the aubergine and chickpea mixture and cook for about 20 minutes until the sauce reduces down slightly. Once you are happy with the consistency, add a squeeze of lemon and three-quarters of the coriander and taste for seasoning. Set aside in a bowl while you rinse and dry the pan.

Add a splash of oil to the clean pan and put the peppers back in. Spoon the chickpea mixture into the peppers and bake until the peppers are soft, about 15–20 minutes. Serve with flatbreads and coconut yoghurt.

SPINACH, WALNUT AND FETA IN THE HOLE

A vegetarian version of toad in the hole without using a vegetarian sausage. Cooked spinach is mixed with walnuts and feta to form patties – and the batter works equally well with sausages of course.

SERVES 4

500g large leaf spinach, thick stalks discarded, or 200g frozen chopped spinach, defrosted

3 spring onions, finely chopped, using as much of the green part as possible

1 clove garlic, crushed or finely grated

150g feta, crumbled

1 tablespoon olive oil

45g walnuts, toasted and chopped

30g panko or other dried breadcrumbs (optional)

FOR THE BATTER

3 eggs

150g plain flour

190ml milk

1 heaped tablespoon wholegrain mustard, dissolved in 65ml warm water

1 tablespoon sunflower or rapeseed oil

Sea salt and black pepper

Start by making the batter, as it benefits from a 15-minute rest before cooking. In a bowl, whisk the eggs until thick and voluminous – use an electric whisk if you have one; otherwise consider it a small cardio workout. Now beat in a third of the flour, followed by a third of the milk, and repeat the process twice more until you have used all the flour and milk. Fold in the mustard and water and season generously.

Preheat the oven to 200°C (180°C fan), gas mark 6. Put a roasting pan, which you have oiled with the sunflower oil, in to heat up.

If using fresh spinach, steam until it wilts, run it under cold water to cool it quickly, then roughly chop. Squeeze the spinach to remove as much water as possible, then place the nice dry spinach in a bowl. Add the spring onions, garlic, feta, olive oil and walnuts and mix thoroughly. Try squeezing some of the mixture together and see if it will form a clump: if it is too wet – this will depend on the type of spinach you have – add the breadcrumbs gradually until it forms a cohesive mass. Divide this into eight equal clumps, shape into balls and flatten with the palm of your hand.

Take the roasting pan out of the oven and turn the oven down to 180°C (160°C fan), gas mark 4. Give the oil a quick swirl to coat the whole pan and add the patties, evenly spaced apart. Now pour in the batter and return the pan to the oven immediately so that the batter can start puffing up straight away.

Bake for 20–25 minutes until set, well risen and golden. Serve immediately. Traditionalists would suggest gravy alongside; alternatively some grilled or roasted tomatoes would be nice.

POTATO, LEEK, SWISS CHARD AND BLUE CHEESE GRATIN

This is a simple vegetarian main course that takes minutes to assemble. I would choose a blue cheese such as bleu d'Auvergne for this – something soft and creamy. A soft goats' cheese would work well, too.

SERVES 4

3 leeks, sliced, using as much of the green part as possible
600g Swiss chard, stalks sliced, leaves torn
200g soft blue cheese, crumbled
1 tablespoon sunflower oil
600g waxy potatoes, cut into ½cm thick slices
Sea salt and black pepper

Preheat the oven to 200°C (180°C fan), gas mark 6.

Bring a large pan of salted water to the boil. Throw in the leeks and chard stalks and blanch for 2 minutes. Add the chard leaves and blanch for another minute. Drain and place in a bowl; don't worry if there is some water clinging to the vegetables. Add two-thirds of the cheese to the hot leek mixture and stir so that it pretty much melts. Season to taste: blue cheese can be salty so you may not need much salt, but a good grinding of black pepper is in order to cut through the richness.

Drizzle the roasting pan with the oil and add half of the potatoes, spread out in a layer and season with salt and pepper. Cover with half of the leek/blue cheese mixture. Now cover with the remaining potatoes, seasoning, and the remaining leeks with any liquid in the bowl. Dot the top with the remaining blue cheese, cover with foil and place in the oven for 35 minutes. Remove the foil and cook for another 10 minutes.

Check it is ready by inserting a sharp knife: it should slide through the potatoes with no resistance. Leave to stand for 5 minutes before serving.

A peppery watercress and almond salad would be a nice accompaniment.

TIP For a vegan version, substitute some chopped toasted almonds and hazelnuts for the cheese and add a good glug of nut oil or olive oil.

PEA AND ARTICHOKE RISOTTO

Cooking rice in the oven like this is not risotto in the strictest sense – although in the north-west coastal strip of Italy, home of pesto, they do cook rice in this way.

SERVES 2

45g butter
2 tablespoons olive oil
2 shallots, finely sliced
Small sprig of rosemary, leaves finely chopped
200g arborio rice
100ml white wine or cider (optional)
600ml boiling vegetable stock
120g frozen peas, defrosted
2 generous tablespoons artichoke purée or 50g artichokes in oil, drained and chopped
30g Parmesan-style vegetarian cheese, grated
Sea salt and black pepper

Preheat the oven to 180°C (160°C fan), gas mark 4, and put a roasting pan in to heat up.

Once the oven is hot, put 30g of the butter, the olive oil, shallots and rosemary into the roasting pan, add a good pinch of salt and place in the oven. After 5 minutes, give the shallots a stir and cook for another 3–5 minutes. They may take on a little bit of colour but cover with foil if they are looking too brown.

Once the shallots are soft, add the rice and stir to coat well with the buttery mixture. If you like, you can add a small glass of white wine or cider and return the pan to the oven for 5 minutes until the wine is absorbed. Add the hot stock, give everything a good stir and bake for 20 minutes.

Add the peas and artichokes and stir well. Return to the oven for 12 minutes. By now the stock will have been absorbed, but the risotto shouldn't be entirely dry.

Stir in the remaining 15g of butter and the cheese, cover with a clean tea towel and leave to settle for 4 minutes. I usually put the plates in the cooling oven to warm up. Serve this comforting supper with a green salad if you wish.

TIP I like using peas and artichokes in this simple recipe because they require very little preparation, but you can use other vegetables. Jerusalem artichokes and some soaked dried wild mushrooms are a winter favourite: you need to slice the artichokes into half moons (I don't bother peeling them as long as they are good and clean) and add them at the same time as the shallots to ensure they are cooked through – I would suggest the same for any root veg. Leafy vegetables could go in later after a couple of minutes in boiling water.

ROAST ASPARAGUS WITH EGG TOASTS

Asparagus is definitely one of my top five vegetables. During its British season it's at its very best and a real treat. The season traditionally starts on St George's Day in April and runs for a good six to eight weeks.

SERVES 4

2 brioche rolls
1 red onion, finely sliced
1½ tablespoons white balsamic vinegar, or cider vinegar and a drizzle of honey
1½ tablespoons olive oil
500g asparagus, trimmed
40g cream cheese with herbs and garlic
4 eggs
200g frozen peas, defrosted
20g Parmesan-style vegetarian cheese, coarsely grated
Sea salt and black pepper

Preheat the oven to 200°C (180°C fan), gas mark 6.

Cut the rolls in half, also cutting off the crown of the top half, to make a stable base. Using a glass or small cup, make an indent in each half roll and remove a little of the crumb to make a hollow to cradle the egg that you will be breaking into it later in the recipe. Place the rolls in the roasting pan and pop them in the oven for about 5 minutes so they dry out a bit and become crisp. Meanwhile, mix the onion with the vinegar and some salt and leave to soften and turn bright pink.

Remove the brioche toasts from the oven and set aside. Add the olive oil and the asparagus to the roasting pan, season generously and shake until the asparagus is well coated with oil. Roast for 8 minutes until the spears are just beginning to yield to the touch, but not too soft. While the asparagus is cooking, spread the cream cheese on the toasts – I use a spoon to do this and encourage the central indent a little more.

Pour some boiling water over the peas to heat them up. Push the asparagus to the sides of the roasting pan, add the toasts and put the pan back in the oven for a few minutes to warm the bread.

With the roasting pan still in the oven, pull it out on its shelf and crack an egg onto each toast, aiming to get the yolk into the central dip, but don't worry – it will be delicious even if the egg is everywhere! Return to the oven for a couple of minutes until the eggs have begun to set. When they have set enough that they are not going to move about, scatter the peas into the pan and season generously. Give the whole lot another 4 minutes or until the egg whites are completely set but the yolks are still runny.

Serve an egg-filled toast on each plate, with some asparagus and peas. Scatter over the red onions and Parmesan-style cheese. Serve immediately.

VICKY'S FILO PIE

I have a great friend called Vicky who gave me this pie for supper recently and I absolutely loved it.
It's a moveable feast in that you can use various vegetables, depending on what you have.

SERVES 4

250g mushrooms, sliced
3½ tablespoons olive oil
2 leeks, sliced, using as
   much of the green part
   as possible
450g spinach
150g Greek yoghurt
180g feta, crumbled
1 teaspoon wholegrain
   mustard
3 sprigs of mint,
   leaves chopped
250g filo pastry
4 eggs
10g Parmesan-style
   vegetarian cheese,
   grated (optional)
Sea salt and black pepper

Preheat the oven to 200°C (180°C fan), gas mark 6.

Put the mushrooms in a roasting pan with 1 tablespoon of the olive oil and a good pinch of salt. Put in the oven for about 10 minutes until soft.

Bring a large pan of salted water to the boil. Throw in the leeks and blanch for 2 minutes. Add the spinach leaves, then immediately drain and refresh in cold water. Drain very thoroughly. I usually leave the vegetables in the colander and press down on them with a small plate or place a small bowl filled with water on top and leave to drain for several minutes.

While the mushrooms are roasting and the leeks and spinach are draining, mix the yoghurt and feta together in a bowl, add the mustard and mint and a good grinding of black pepper. Taste and add salt if necessary.

Once the leek mixture is thoroughly drained, add the mushrooms and the yoghurt mixture, mix thoroughly and taste for seasoning.

Rinse and dry the roasting pan. Brush the pan with oil and line with filo pastry; it can hang over the sides of the pan, but trim if there is a lot of excess pastry. Brush the pastry with oil and add another layer of filo. Repeat until you have used four sheets of filo.

Add the vegetable mixture and make four hollows, evenly spaced in the pie, one towards each corner. Crack an egg into each hollow.

Cover with another sheet of filo pastry, fold in any overhang and brush with the remaining oil. Score the top in a diamond pattern and scatter with the Parmesan-style cheese, if using. Cook for 30 minutes until golden and crisp. Serve hot.

BAKED ANGEL HAIR PASTA WITH BROCCOLI AND GREEN BEANS

This is based on the Catalan dish fideuà: essentially it's a paella made with thin noodles instead of rice. You will need a second roasting pan to roast the broccoli and green beans.

SERVES 4

VEGAN

3 tablespoons extra
   virgin olive oil
2 small onions,
   finely sliced
4 cloves garlic – 3 finely
   sliced, 1 finely grated
1½ teaspoons cayenne
   pepper
1½ teaspoons smoked
   paprika
1 teaspoon fennel
   seeds, ground
1 bay leaf
A few sprigs of thyme
500g angel hair pasta
   (capelli d'angelo)

Preheat the oven to 220°C (200°C fan), gas mark 7. Put a roasting pan in to heat up with 1½ tablespoons of the olive oil.

Once hot, add the onions and a pinch of salt and cook for 5 minutes. Add the sliced garlic, cayenne, paprika, fennel seeds, bay leaf and thyme and cook for a further 2 minutes.

Meanwhile, break up the angel hair a bit. When the onion is softened and lightly golden, add the pasta to the roasting pan and cook for 7 minutes, shaking the pan halfway through.

Put another roasting pan with the remaining olive oil into the oven.

Add the peppers to the pasta along with the butter beans, tomato juice and 300ml of the hot stock. Ensure that the pasta is immersed in the liquid and return to the oven for a few minutes. Once the stock is bubbling, add the saffron strands and water, if using. Give everything a stir and ensure that the pasta is covered with liquid with a couple of centimetres to spare, adding more hot stock if necessary.

¼ x 450g jar roasted
  peppers
400g tin butter beans,
  drained and rinsed
300ml tomato juice
500ml boiling vegetable
  stock
Pinch of saffron soaked
  in 100ml warm water
  (optional)
1 head broccoli, broken
  into small florets
100g green beans
Grated zest and juice
  of ½ lemon
Generous handful of
  parsley, finely chopped
Sea salt

While the pasta is cooking, throw the broccoli and green beans into the second roasting pan, toss well to coat with oil and add a good pinch of salt. Roast for 15 minutes.

Check the pasta after 7 minutes: it may need another 5–7 minutes until perfectly al dente with just a little liquid remaining. Season to taste.

Remove from the oven and leave to stand while the broccoli and beans finish cooking. When the vegetables are done, squeeze the lemon juice over them and scatter over the parsley, grated garlic and lemon zest; toss it through thoroughly. To serve, spoon out the fideuà and top with some of the broccoli and beans.

LENTILS, CRISPY KALE AND HALLOUMI

Tinned lentils are a brilliant cupboard staple. There is nothing more nourishing than a bowl of lentils with plenty of vegetables. Finish with kale and halloumi – cooked in a second roasting pan – for a bit of texture.

SERVES 4

5 tablespoons olive oil
2 onions, sliced
2 leeks, finely sliced, using as much as of the green part as possible
3 celery sticks, finely sliced
3 carrots, cut in half lengthways and sliced into fine half moons
3 cloves garlic, sliced
1 heaped teaspoon chilli flakes
2 tablespoons sherry vinegar
400g tin green lentils, drained and rinsed
400g tin cherry tomatoes
400ml boiling vegetable stock
200g kale, thick stalks removed, washed and thoroughly dried
2 x 250g blocks halloumi, cut into cubes
Sea salt and black pepper

Preheat the oven to 190°C (170°C fan), gas mark 5. Put a roasting pan in to heat up with 2 tablespoons of the olive oil.

Once hot, add the onions and a good pinch of salt and cook for about 10 minutes until softened and lightly golden. Add another tablespoon of oil, the leeks, celery and carrots and mix thoroughly, then return to the oven for another 10 minutes so that the vegetables start to get some golden brown edges.

Add the garlic, chilli and sherry vinegar, give everything a good stir and return to the oven for 5 minutes. Next add the lentils, cherry tomatoes and hot stock, stir and return to the oven for 30 minutes.

Meanwhile, place the kale in a bowl with 1 tablespoon of the remaining olive oil and some salt and pepper and rub the oil thoroughly into the kale while breaking it up into bite-sized pieces. Place the kale in a single layer in a large roasting pan. Put the halloumi into the same bowl with the final 1 tablespoon of olive oil and toss it about to ensure it is well coated, then scatter among the kale.

After the lentils have been in the oven for about 10 minutes, place the roasting pan of kale on the top shelf of the oven and cook for 20 minutes until the kale is crisp and the halloumi golden.

Taste the lentils for seasoning, bearing in mind that halloumi can be quite salty. Serve the lentils with the cheese and kale crisps on top.

TIP For a vegan version, omit the halloumi – you could add some pumpkin seeds to the kale for extra protein and texture.

BAKED FARINATA, RED PEPPER AND COURGETTE WITH OLIVE DRESSING

Farinata is a sort of pancake made with chickpea flour, originating in Genoa in north-west Italy. For a non-vegan version, you could serve it with some soft goats' cheese underneath the olive dressing.

SERVES 4

VEGAN

3 tablespoons olive oil
3 courgettes, sliced into
 3cm thick circles
2 red peppers, cut in half
 lengthways, then each
 half into 4 long pieces
2 red onions, sliced into
 2cm thick circles
1 large sprig of rosemary,
 leaves roughly chopped
150g chickpea flour
½ teaspoon baking powder
400g tin chickpeas,
 drained, reserving the
 liquid, and rinsed
Sea salt and black pepper

FOR THE OLIVE DRESSING
120g pimento-stuffed
 olives
Small handful of basil,
 roughly torn
1 clove garlic, crushed
1 small red chilli, deseeded
 and chopped
Grated zest of ½ lemon,
 juice of 1 lemon
1 tablespoon olive oil

Preheat the oven to 200°C (220°C fan), gas mark 6. Put a roasting pan in to heat up with 2 tablespoons of the olive oil.

When the oil is hot, add the courgettes, peppers and onions, the rosemary and plenty of seasoning. Shake to coat all the vegetables in the oil and roast for about 25 minutes until they are soft and lightly golden.

Meanwhile, make the batter: put the flour, baking powder and 1 teaspoon of salt into a bowl, make a well in the centre and add the liquid from the chickpeas made up to 300ml with warm water, whisking until smooth. Set aside.

When the vegetables are soft, take the pan out of the oven and turn the oven up to 220°C (200°C fan), gas mark 7. Add the chickpeas to the pan with the remaining olive oil, stir everything together and then pour in the batter. Return the pan to the oven until the batter is set and crisp and golden brown around the edges – this will take about 20 minutes, but check after 15 minutes and cover with foil if it is browning too much and not setting.

While the farinata is cooking, make the dressing. Put the olives, basil, garlic, chilli and lemon zest into a food processor and whizz to a rough paste. Add the olive oil and lemon juice and season to taste.

When the farinata is set, take it out of the oven and let it stand for 5 minutes, then turn out onto a board and cut into squares. Serve with some of the olive dressing on top. This would be delicious with a tomato salad.

CAULIFLOWER KUKU

Kuku is the name for a Persian-style omelette. There are many versions, I am particularly keen on this one, with cauliflower, spices and raisins. It's great served cold for a picnic or warm as a nibble with drinks.

SERVES 4

1 small cauliflower,
  broken into small
  florets
4 spring onions,
  finely sliced
2 tablespoons olive oil
1 tablespoon ground
  rice or cornflour
5 eggs
½ teaspoon baking
  powder
1½ teaspoons turmeric
1 teaspoon ground cumin
1 teaspoon smoked
  paprika
Few sprigs of dill,
  finely chopped
Small handful of
  coriander, chopped
20g butter
2 cloves garlic, crushed
  or finely grated
40g raisins
Sea salt and black pepper

Preheat the oven to 200°C (180°C fan), gas mark 6.

In a roasting pan, toss the cauliflower, spring onions and olive oil together with plenty of salt and pepper and roast for 15 minutes.

Meanwhile, mix the ground rice or cornflour with some boiling water to make a pourable paste. Whisk the eggs in a bowl, then whisk in the rice or cornflour paste, the baking powder, spices, herbs, 100ml water, salt and pepper.

Add the butter, garlic and raisins to the roasting pan and toss together with the cauliflower. Return to the oven for a few minutes, then add the egg mixture. Turn the oven down to 180°C (160°C fan), gas mark 4, and cook the omelette for about 20 minutes or until set. Serve with flatbreads and maybe a simple carrot salad.

FRENCH ONION WELSH RAREBIT

This recipe is a mixture of French onion soup, which is such a comforting dish, with the added goodness of cabbage among the slow-cooked onions, and a Welsh rarebit topping. What a combo!

SERVES 6

6 onions, cut in half and
   then into wedges
4 cloves garlic, sliced
3 sprigs of thyme
1½ tablespoons balsamic
   vinegar
2 tablespoons sunflower oil
1 small pointed (sweetheart
   or hispi) cabbage, cut in
   half lengthways and then
   into 2cm wide ribbons
20g butter
100ml white wine or
   cider (optional)
100ml vegetable stock
Sea salt and black pepper

FOR THE TOPPING

6 slices of white bread or
   18 slices of baguette,
   about 2–3cm thick
100g mature Cheddar,
   grated
50g Gruyère, grated
1½ tablespoons
   Worcestershire sauce
1 teaspoon English mustard
½ teaspoon cayenne pepper
1 egg, beaten
3 tablespoons crème fraîche

Preheat the oven to 180°C (160°C fan), gas mark 4. Put the bread slices in to toast while the oven is heating up: you want them to be crisp but still yielding. Set aside.

In a roasting pan, toss the onions, garlic and thyme with the balsamic vinegar, oil, and a generous pinch of salt. Cover with foil and cook for about 25 minutes until the onions are soft and sweet; after 10 minutes, stir and add a cup of boiling water.

When the onions are soft, take the pan out of the oven and turn the oven up to 200°C (180°C fan), gas mark 6. Remove the foil, add the cabbage, butter, a good grinding of black pepper and a little more salt and give everything a good stir. Return to the oven for 7 minutes until the onions absorb their cooking liquid and brown a little.

Add the wine or cider, if using, and stock (adding an extra 100ml of stock if you didn't use wine) and return to the oven for a few minutes to heat the liquid.

While the onions are cooking, prepare the topping: mix the cheeses with the Worcestershire sauce, mustard, cayenne, egg and crème fraîche. Spread this mixture onto the toasts.

Take the roasting pan out of the oven and pick out any thyme stalks you can see. Pop the toasts on top and return to the oven until the cheese melts and the top is golden and bubbling.

Spoon into warm soup plates and serve immediately.

TIP For a vegetarian version, omit the Gruyère cheese and Worcestershire sauce, or use vegetarian substitutes.

TOMATO AND PEPPER TIAN

My friends the Russell family are keen tian makers. They have several variations, usually based on green vegetables, and all are delicious. This is my red version.

SERVES 4

2 large red peppers,
 deseeded and cut
 into 3cm chunks
2 banana shallots,
 cut into quarters
 lengthways
2 sprigs of thyme –
 lemon thyme if you
 can get it
2 tablespoons olive oil
500g cherry tomatoes
200ml boiling vegetable
 stock
2 eggs, beaten
40g Parmesan-style
 vegetarian cheese,
 grated
180g cooked rice
20g fresh or dried
 breadcrumbs
Sea salt and black pepper

Preheat the oven to 200°C (180°C fan), gas mark 6.

Toss the peppers, shallots and thyme together in a roasting pan with the olive oil, season well and place in the oven for 15 minutes, shaking the pan halfway through the cooking time.

Add the tomatoes and cook for another 15 minutes.

Crush the tomatoes with the back of a spoon, add the hot stock and cook for another 10 minutes.

Meanwhile, fold the eggs and all but a tablespoon of the cheese into the rice.

By now the peppers and shallots will be soft and there should be plenty of liquid in the roasting pan. Stir in the rice mixture, scatter over the breadcrumbs and the remaining Parmesan-style cheese and bake for 10–15 minutes until golden. Serve hot or at room temperature, with a green salad.

ROOT VEGETABLE RÖSTI WITH HAZELNUT GREMOLATA

A lovely winter warmer of a dish. Sometimes I might put a poached egg with it, but it's great as is. It also works well as a side dish with sausages or chops.

SERVES 4

200g floury potatoes, scrubbed, not peeled, coarsely grated

150g each of parsnips, sweet potatoes and carrots, peeled and coarsely grated

1 large onion, grated

1 sprig of rosemary, leaves finely chopped

1 tablespoon plain four

40g butter, melted

1½ tablespoons sunflower oil

Sea salt and black pepper

FOR THE GREMOLATA

30g hazelnuts, chopped

1 clove garlic, grated

Small handful of parsley, finely chopped

Small sprig of sage, leaves finely chopped

Grated zest of ½ lemon

10g Parmesan-style vegetarian cheese, finely grated

Preheat the oven to 190°C (170°C fan), gas mark 5. Put the hazelnuts in a roasting pan and put them in the oven to toast gently as the oven heats up. Keep a close eye on them as they can burn very quickly. Once they are golden, remove from the roasting pan and set aside.

Mix together all the root vegetables with the onion, rosemary, flour and plenty of seasoning. Fold in the melted butter and stir to ensure all the roots are well coated.

Wipe the roasting pan with FSC kitchen paper, then return it to the oven with the oil for 5–7 minutes until it is nice and hot. Swirl the pan to coat it thoroughly with the oil and tip in the root vegetables. Shake to level them out and return to the oven for 35–45 minutes until the vegetables are cooked through and crisp on top. Check from time to time: if they are getting too brown you can cover the pan with foil.

Meanwhile, mix together the ingredients for the gremolata topping.

To test the rösti, insert the point of a sharp knife, which should meet no resistance. Remove from the oven and leave to rest for a few minutes. Scatter the top with the gremolata and serve straight from the roasting pan. I often accompany this with charred cabbage (page 108).

TIP For a vegan version, use a nut or olive oil instead of butter and omit the cheese.

BUTTER BEANS, LEEKS AND RICOTTA WITH A CRISPY KALE TOP

When I first thought about this dish I was imagining a sort of lasagne, but I have become so addicted to crispy kale that I thought it would make a great topping for a baked dish – much lighter and quicker!

SERVES 2

2½ tablespoons olive oil
2 leeks, sliced, using as
    much of the green part
    as possible
400g tin butter beans,
    drained and rinsed
2 tablespoons cider
    vinegar
150ml boiling vegetable
    stock
200g kale, thick stalks
    removed, washed,
    thoroughly dried
200g ricotta
3 generous tablespoons
    vegetarian pesto
20g pine nuts
20g Parmesan-style
    vegetarian cheese,
    grated
Sea salt and black pepper

Preheat the oven to 190°C (170°C fan), gas mark 5. Put a roasting pan in to heat up with 1½ tablespoons of the olive oil.

When hot, add the leeks and plenty of seasoning, and place in the oven for 7 minutes. At the same time, put the butter beans into some boiling water so they start to heat up. Splash the vinegar in with the leeks and place in the oven to evaporate for a couple of minutes. Now drain the butter beans and add them to the roasting pan, along with the stock. Return to the oven for 10 minutes.

Meanwhile, place the kale in a bowl with the remaining olive oil and some salt and pepper and rub the oil thoroughly into the kale while breaking it up into bite-sized pieces. Put the ricotta in a bowl and season it well.

Stir the pesto into the leek and bean mixture. Blob the ricotta all over the mixture and scatter over the kale. Return to the oven for about 15–20 minutes until the kale is starting to crisp up. Add the pine nuts and cheese and cook for a further 5 minutes. Serve hot.

TIP For a vegan version, omit the ricotta and use a vegan pesto.

BAKED PEARL BARLEY, PEAS, BEANS AND GREEN SAUCE

Pearl barley is quite an old-fashioned ingredient, often used in stews – it has a delicious nutty flavour and it bakes well.

SERVES 4

VEGAN

2 tablespoons olive oil
1 large onion, sliced
1 leek, sliced, using as much of the green part as possible
200g pearl barley
850ml boiling vegetable stock
120g frozen peas, defrosted
120g frozen edamame beans, defrosted
100g baby spinach
Sea salt and black pepper

FOR THE GREEN SAUCE
Generous handful of parsley, chopped
6 sprigs of mint, leaves chopped
2 cloves garlic, crushed
1 tablespoon Dijon mustard
1 tablespoon red wine vinegar
6 tablespoons extra virgin olive oil
2 tablespoons capers

Preheat the oven to 200°C (180°C fan), gas mark 6. Put a roasting pan in to heat up with the olive oil.

When hot, add the onion and leek and plenty of seasoning and place in the oven to soften for 15 minutes, stirring a couple of times.

Add the barley and cook for about 4 minutes, then add the boiling stock and cook for 25 minutes.

Meanwhile, make the green sauce. If you would like a very smooth sauce, put everything except the olive oil and capers into a blender or food processor and whizz to a paste – you may need to add some of the oil to help the process on its way. Add the remaining oil with the motor running. Finally fold in the capers, either on pulse or by hand. For a more rustic version, whisk everything together by hand.

After 25 minutes, add the peas and edamame beans to the barley and return to the oven for 10 minutes. The barley should be quite moist – if necessary add some boiling water.

When the barley is soft and nutty-tasting, fold in the spinach and a couple of tablespoons of the green sauce. Leave to stand for 5 minutes before serving with the remaining green sauce in a bowl.

ROAST SQUASH, CHESTNUTS AND MUSHROOMS WITH GNOCCHI

A lovely autumnal combination for a warming quick supper.

SERVES 2

2 tablespoons olive oil

300g squash, peeled, deseeded and cut into 2cm chunks

1 red onion, cut into six wedges

Couple of sprigs of sage, leaves chopped

200g mushrooms – I like to use a mixture of oyster, chestnut and button

200g fresh gnocchi

50g peeled cooked chestnuts, roughly chopped

2 tablespoons balsamic vinegar

20g Parmesan-style vegetarian cheese, grated

Sea salt and black pepper

Sage leaves, to garnish

Preheat the oven to 200°C (180°C fan), gas mark 6. Put a roasting pan in to heat up with the olive oil.

Toss the squash, onion and sage together with plenty of seasoning and throw into the hot roasting pan. Stir until everything is coated with oil and roast for 15 minutes.

Add the mushrooms and cook for another 15 minutes.

Meanwhile, drop the gnocchi into boiling water for a minute to heat through. Drain, mix with the chestnuts and add to the roasting pan. Toss everything together well and add the balsamic vinegar. Return to the oven for 7 minutes.

Stir in the cheese. Taste for seasoning, garnish with a couple of sage leaves and serve immediately.

TIP For a vegan version, omit the cheese and take care to check the ingredients list of the gnocchi as some brands use egg.

SIDES

CHARRED CABBAGE WITH CHILLI AND SHERRY VINEGAR

Unbelievably simple, this dish is addictive! It's great with sausages, pork chops or gammon steaks. A generous grating of cheese on top and a buttery baked potato served alongside makes a good vegetarian supper.

SERVES 2–3

VEGAN

1 pointed (sweetheart or hispi) cabbage, about 500g
3 tablespoons olive oil
1 tablespoon sherry vinegar
Generous pinch of chilli flakes
Sea salt

Preheat the oven to 200°C (180°C fan), gas mark 6, with a large roasting pan in it.

Cut the cabbage lengthways into six wedges, discarding any unwanted core. Give it a little dunk in water, then shake off the excess.

Oil the hot roasting pan with 1 tablespoon of the olive oil, add the cabbage and the other 2 tablespoons of olive oil and a good pinch of salt. Pop into the oven for 15 minutes.

After this time the cabbage will be soft, with wonderful caramelised outer leaves. As soon as you take the very hot pan out of the oven, splash in the vinegar – it will almost completely evaporate. Scatter over the chilli flakes and give the whole pan a good shake. Serve immediately.

ROASTED OKRA

*Okra makes an unusual and very easy side dish, good with any grilled
fish or meat. I use urfa chilli for this, but any chilli flakes will do.*

SERVES 4

VEGAN

2 tablespoons olive oil
600g okra, tops removed
1 bunch of spring onions
1 teaspoon onion seeds
½ teaspoon chilli flakes
Small handful of
   coriander, chopped
Juice of ½ lime

Preheat the oven to 200°C (180°C fan), gas mark 6. Put a roasting pan
in to heat up with the olive oil.

When the oil is hot, slice the okra and spring onions in half lengthways,
throw in the roasting pan with the onion seeds and chilli and toss
everything about until well mixed. Return to the oven, ensuring the
okra is in a single layer as much as possible, and roast for 25 minutes
until crisp and golden.

Scatter over the coriander and lime juice and serve.

ROAST CELERIAC WITH WHOLEGRAIN MUSTARD AND ROSEMARY

*Celeriac has an earthy sweet flavour that goes brilliantly with mustard. Celeriac remoulade is a classic
French salad of shredded celeriac with a mustardy dressing, and this is my variation on that theme.*

SERVES 4

VEGAN

2 tablespoons olive oil
1 large celeriac
1 large sprig of rosemary,
   leaves finely chopped
2 large tablespoons
   wholegrain mustard
2 cloves garlic, sliced
Sea salt and black pepper

Preheat the oven to 190°C (170°C fan), gas mark 5. Put a roasting pan
in to heat up with the olive oil. Peel the celariac and cut into 2cm cubes.

When the oven is hot, pop the celeriac and rosemary into the pan, season
generously and stir well; the celeriac should be in a single layer. Roast for
10 minutes until the celeriac is starting to colour. Give it a good stir and
then cover the pan with foil. Roast for another 20 minutes, shaking the
pan halfway through, until the celeriac is soft.

Remove the foil, stir in the mustard and garlic and return to the oven for
another 10 minutes. Taste for seasoning and serve hot.

BROCCOLI 'RICE', FLAGEOLET BEANS AND ROAST VEGETABLES

You can use any vegetables you like in this recipe, but bear in mind that some will need more roasting than others. They should all be soft and golden brown before you add the beans and broccoli.

SERVES 4

VEGAN

30g pine nuts

350g broccoli, broken
　　into florets, stem
　　reserved

4 tablespoons olive oil

1 head fennel, fronds
　　reserved, cut in half
　　lengthways, thick core
　　removed, cut into
　　3mm-thick slices

4 spring onions, cut into
　　3cm lengths, using as
　　much of the green
　　part as possible

2 courgettes, cut in half
　　lengthways then cut
　　into 3cm lengths

Small handful of parsley,
　　finely chopped

Grated zest of ½ lemon,
　　juice of 1 lemon

1 large clove garlic,
　　finely grated

400g tin flageolet beans,
　　drained and rinsed

150ml boiling water
　　or vegetable stock

Sea salt and black pepper

Preheat the oven to 190°C (170°C fan), gas mark 5. Put the pine nuts in a roasting pan and put them in the oven to toast gently as the oven heats up. Watch them like a hawk as they can burn very quickly. Once the pine nuts are golden, remove from the roasting pan and set aside.

Put the broccoli florets in a food processor and whizz to small confetti-sized pieces; set aside. Trim the broccoli stem of any stringy or hard outer skin; the inside is tender and delicious, so cut the stem into slices the thickness of a pound coin.

Add 2 tablespoons of the olive oil to the roasting pan along with the broccoli stem, fennel, spring onions and courgettes. Add 3 tablespoons of hot water (this will evaporate, and ensures the fennel doesn't get wrinkly), season generously and roast for about 15 minutes, shaking halfway through.

Meanwhile, chop the fennel fronds and mix with the parsley, lemon zest, garlic and cooled pine nuts.

After 15 minutes the vegetables should be soft and golden brown – if not, return to the oven for a few minutes. Add the flageolet beans, broccoli 'rice' and the remaining olive oil, then add the hot water or stock and stir to ensure everything is well coated with oil. Return to the oven for 15 minutes.

Squeeze over the lemon juice, scatter with the pine nut mixture and serve.

BAKED BEETROOT WITH HAZELNUT DRESSING

New-season beetroot are perfectly complemented by this herby hazelnut dressing, which also goes well with goats' cheese.

SERVES 4

VEGAN

650g raw beetroot
2 tablespoons olive oil
Sea salt and black pepper

FOR THE HAZELNUT DRESSING
150ml olive oil
100ml verjuice, or
   60ml cider vinegar
   plus 40ml apple juice
1 clove garlic, crushed
125g hazelnuts, skinless,
   toasted and roughly
   chopped
125g whole blanched
   almonds, toasted and
   roughly chopped
Generous handful of
   flat-leaf parsley,
   chopped
5 sprigs of basil, leaves
   chopped

Preheat the oven to 180°C (160°C fan), gas mark 4.

Wash the beetroot thoroughly, leaving the skins on – beetroot is easier to peel once cooked. Place in a roasting pan – they should fit snugly – and toss with the olive oil and plenty of salt and pepper. Pour in some water to cover the base of the pan by about 1cm. Cover with foil and roast for 45–60 minutes, or until a knife can slide easily into the largest beetroot.

While the beetroot bake, make the dressing. Whisk the olive oil, verjuice and garlic together until thoroughly mixed. Stir in the nuts and herbs and season to taste with salt and pepper.

Once the beetroot is done, leave it until cool enough to handle, then peel: the skins should slip off easily. Cut the beetroot into bite-sized chunks and toss with enough dressing to coat generously. Serve warm or at room temperature.

Any leftover dressing will keep well in the fridge for several days; the herbs may discolour a little, but you can add a few fresh herbs, if you wish.

TIP Verjuice is a gentle acidulant, usually made from unripe grapes. It is fruitier and sweeter than vinegar, so if you can't get hold of it, I suggest substituting a mixture of apple juice and vinegar.

BAKED ROOTS WITH LANCASHIRE CHEESE CRUMBS

Lancashire cheese is a good foil to the robust, slightly sharp flavours of swede and turnip.
The carrots and parsnips bring sweetness to this wonderful autumn/winter warmer.

SERVES 4

2 tablespoons sunflower
  or rapeseed oil
1 small swede,
  peeled and cut
  into 3cm chunks
3 parsnips, peeled and
  cut into 3cm pieces
2 carrots, peeled and
  cut into 3cm pieces
2 turnips, peeled and
  cut into 3cm chunks
2 banana shallots, peeled
  and cut into sixths
  lengthways
40g panko or other
  dried breadcrumbs
30g Lancashire cheese,
  crumbled
3 sprigs of sage, leaves
  finely chopped
1 tablespoon sherry
  vinegar
Sea salt and black pepper

Preheat the oven to 190°C (170°C fan), gas mark 5. Put a large roasting pan in to heat up with the oil.

Once the pan is hot, add the vegetables, season generously and toss to ensure everything is well coated with oil. Bake for 35–40 minutes until the vegetables are soft and have golden edges here and there.

Meanwhile, mix together the breadcrumbs, cheese and sage.

Once the vegetables are done, splash in the sherry vinegar and scatter over the crumbs, then return to the oven for 5 minutes until the crumbs are brown and melty. Serve hot.

BAKED BABY CARROTS AND HARISSA

Harissa is a North African chilli paste that goes really well with carrots (I like the rose version). This dish would be good on a table of salads and is great for vegans: try it in a flatbread with some pickles and toasted nuts.

SERVES 4

VEGAN

2 tablespoons olive oil
500g baby carrots
1 tablespoon harissa
Juice of 1 lime
Small handful of
  coriander, chopped
Sea salt and black pepper

Preheat the oven to 180°C (160°C fan), gas mark 4. Put a roasting pan in to heat up with the olive oil. Once hot, add the carrots, season well and give everything a good stir.

Roast for about 25 minutes, until the carrots are just tender, but not too soft; give them a stir halfway through, which is a good opportunity to test them and adjust timings. Once the carrots are done, add the harissa, lime juice and coriander and mix together thoroughly. Serve hot.

OVEN-BRAISED BEANS WITH SMOKED PAPRIKA AND THYME

This works well with any beans, so you can decide which will go best with whatever else you plan to serve. I've used butter beans, which are great with sausages.

SERVES 4

2 tablespoons olive oil
20g butter
125g banana
   shallots, sliced
4 sprigs of thyme
1 bay leaf
2 generous teaspoons
   smoked paprika
1 leek, sliced, using as
   much of the green
   part as possible
1 carrot, sliced
1 celery stick, sliced
1 tablespoon red
   wine vinegar
4 large cloves garlic,
   crushed or grated
400g tin butter beans,
   drained and rinsed
200ml boiling vegetable
   stock
Sea salt and black pepper

Preheat the oven to 180°C (160°C fan), gas mark 4. Put a roasting pan in to heat up with the oil and butter.

Once hot, add the shallots, thyme, bay leaf, paprika and a generous pinch of salt and place in the oven until they soften – this will take about 15 minutes – shaking the pan halfway through.

Add the leek, carrot and celery and stir well to coat with the fat, add another good pinch of salt and return to the oven for 12 minutes until everything has softened. A little bit of colour is fine, but if the vegetables are looking too brown, cover the pan with foil.

Add the vinegar and then the garlic and beans and stir thoroughly, pour in the stock and return to the oven for 5–7 minutes. Give the beans a stir and taste for seasoning.

POTATO AND TOMATO GRATIN

This is a summer version of a gratin dauphinoise, with tomatoes and lemon thyme instead of cream.
It goes really well with a barbecue and is equally good hot or at room temperature.

SERVES 4–6

3–4 tablespoons olive oil

20g butter

500g plum tomatoes,
   sliced

2 red onions, finely sliced

3 cloves garlic, crushed
   or grated

3 sprigs of lemon thyme
   or regular thyme

600g potatoes,
   thinly sliced

50g Parmesan or
   Parmesan-style
   vegetarian cheese,
   grated

400g boiling vegetable
   stock

30g fresh or dried
   breadcrumbs

Sea salt and black pepper

Preheat the oven to 180°C (160°C fan), gas mark 4. Put a roasting pan into the oven with 1 tablespoon of the olive oil and half the butter.

In a bowl, mix the tomatoes with the onions, garlic, thyme and plenty of salt and pepper.

Once the butter has melted, remove the roasting pan from the oven and brush the butter all over the pan. Put a third of the potatoes into the pan in an even layer and season well. Scatter over half the tomato mixture, including half of the liquid which will have accumulated in the bowl and 1 tablespoon of olive oil, then scatter over a third of the Parmesan. Next add another third of the potatoes and seasoning, then the remaining tomato mixture and juice with another tablespoon of oil, then another third of the Parmesan. Add the potatoes and season well, then pour in the hot stock.

Scatter the breadcrumbs and the remaining Parmesan over the top and dot with the remaining butter and a drizzle of olive oil. Cover with foil and place in the oven for 35 minutes, by which time the potatoes should be starting to give when pierced with a sharp knife. Remove the foil and return to the oven for 10–15 minutes until the potatoes are tender. Leave to stand for 5–10 minutes before serving.

TIP For a vegan version, substitute the butter for more oil and instead of Parmesan use Panko breadcrumbs through each of the layers.

RED CABBAGE WITH CHESTNUT AND APPLE

Red cabbage is such a comforting winter dish and it goes wonderfully with everything from baked potatoes to roast pheasant. This just goes in the oven and does its thing while you do yours.

SERVES 4–6

VEGAN

1 red cabbage, cut in
  half, cored and sliced
3 onions, finely sliced
2 tablespoons sunflower
  or rapeseed oil
3 tablespoons nut or
  olive oil
2 apples – I like
  red-skinned ones –
  quartered, cored
  and sliced
100g peeled cooked
  chestnuts, chopped
3 tablespoons cider
  vinegar
1 cinnamon stick
1 tablespoon dark
  brown sugar
Sea salt and black pepper

Put the cabbage and onions in a large bowl, sprinkle with plenty of salt and leave them to soften for at least 20 minutes or longer if you have time.

Preheat the oven to 180°C (160°C fan), gas mark 4. Put a roasting pan in to heat up with the two types of oil.

Mix the cabbage, onions, apples and all the remaining ingredients together. Add to the hot roasting pan and stir to ensure everything is well coated with the fat. Press down to an even layer, cover with foil and place in the oven for about an hour, shaking everything about from time to time. If there is a lot of liquid, remove the foil for the last 20 minutes or so. The end result should be soft and sweet with not too much liquid. Taste for seasoning before serving.

OVEN-BAKED MUSHROOMS À LA GRECQUE

À la grecque is a proper old French treatment of vegetables, served cold as a first course. This is a simple oven version. It does improve if left overnight, but is delicious eaten straight away with bread to mop up the tasty sauce.

SERVES 4

2 teaspoons
    coriander seeds
3 tablespoons olive oil
500g chestnut
    mushrooms, wiped
    clean and halved
4 spring onions, chopped
    into 4cm lengths
1 small head fennel,
    trimmed and thinly
    sliced
1 bay leaf
2 cloves garlic,
    crushed or grated
3 tablespoons white
    wine (optional)
1 teaspoon honey
1 tablespoon tomato
    purée
120ml boiling vegetable
    stock
2 tablespoons white
    wine vinegar
Few sprigs of tarragon
    or parsley, leaves
    finely chopped
Sea salt and black pepper

Preheat the oven to 180°C (160°C fan), gas mark 4. Put the coriander seeds in a roasting pan and put them in the oven to toast gently as the oven heats up. Once toasted, tip them onto a board and roughly crush the seeds while still warm.

Now put 2 tablespoons of the olive oil in the roasting pan and add the mushrooms, spring onions, fennel and bay leaf, mix thoroughly and put in the oven for 15 minutes to soften. The mushrooms usually exude quite a lot of liquid at this stage.

While they are cooking, mix the coriander seeds, the remaining olive oil, garlic, white wine (if using), honey, tomato purée and stock together and keep hot. If you are not using wine, add another 3 tablespoons of hot stock.

After 15 minutes, turn the oven up to 200°C (180°C fan), gas mark 6. Add the vinegar to the mushrooms and stir well. Return to the oven for about 10 minutes until the juices are reabsorbed into the mushrooms.

Add the hot stock mixture and cook for a further 15 minutes. By this time the liquid should have reduced down to make a nice rich sauce over the mushrooms. Fish out the bay leaf, stir in the tarragon or parsley, taste for seasoning and serve.

ROAST CAULIFLOWER AND BROCCOLI WITH TOASTED ALMOND DRESSING

Roasting broccoli and cauliflower is a dream, giving golden crisp edges and tender insides. The almond dressing works so well with the broccoli and cauliflower and is also good as a dip for crudités.

SERVES 4

VEGAN

1 head broccoli,
    broken into florets
1 small cauliflower,
    broken into florets
2 tablespoons olive oil
Sea salt and black pepper

FOR THE ALMOND

DRESSING

150g skin-on almonds,
    or a mixture of skin
    on and blanched
1 tablespoon olive oil,
    for drizzling
1 large clove garlic,
    peeled
2 tablespoons
    sherry vinegar
75ml extra virgin
    olive oil

Preheat the oven to 200°C (180°C fan), gas mark 6. Put the almonds in a large roasting pan with a drizzle of olive oil and a scattering of salt and put them in the oven to toast gently as the oven heats. Keep an eye on them as they can burn very quickly. You want them to be golden inside and you can crush one to check; they will carry on colouring as they cool. Remove from the roasting pan and set aside.

Once the almonds are done and the oven is hot, put the broccoli and cauliflower into the roasting pan with the olive oil and plenty of salt and pepper; toss to coat them with the oil. Roast for 15–20 minutes until the vegetables are just tender, with some nice golden brown edges.

Meanwhile, while the almonds are still warm, put them in a food processor and whizz until the oil is starting to come out of them. Add the garlic and a couple of tablespoons of boiling water to help the process along, and keep going until you have an almost smooth purée. Add the sherry vinegar and gradually add the extra virgin olive oil, a little at a time. Taste and adjust the seasoning and whizz once again. If very thick, add some more boiling water: you are looking for a coating or dipping consistency.

Once the vegetables are ready, spoon over the dressing and serve immediately.

SWEET

CHOCOLATE BANANA TAHINI BROWNIE

Imagine this warm with some cream or ice cream on top! The tahini gives the brownie a distinctive flavour and the banana keeps it wonderfully moist.

SERVES 8–10

300g dark chocolate
75g butter
100g tahini, plus a
  generous tablespoon
  to finish
3 eggs
200g soft light
  brown sugar
2 ripe bananas, mashed
80g rye flour
1 teaspoon sesame seeds
Sea salt

Preheat the oven to 180°C (160°C fan), gas mark 4. Line a small roasting pan or baking tin (approx. 30 x 20cm) with a reusable silicone baking sheet.

Melt the chocolate, butter and tahini in a heatproof bowl over a pan of barely simmering water.

Meanwhile, whisk the eggs, sugar and a pinch of salt together until light and fluffy. Fold in the mashed bananas, then the melted chocolate mix. You will notice that the mixture starts to thicken a little. When everything is thoroughly mixed, carefully fold in the flour until fully incorporated.

Turn into the prepared tin and drizzle the remaining tablespoon of tahini all over the top. Then sprinkle over the sesame seeds.

Bake for 25–30 minutes until the brownie is just set – it should still feel soft and moist. Leave the tin on a wire rack to cool for an hour or so.

TIP These brownies could be made gluten-free by substituting the rye flour for a gluten-free flour.

RICE PUDDING WITH A DIFFERENCE

I have been making this rice pudding for years using almond milk, but oat milk is equally good. Maple syrup and lemon zest give a delicious caramelised flavour. For a vegan version, omit the butter or use almond butter instead.

SERVES 4

150g short grain rice
1 litre almond or oat milk
4 tablespoons maple
    syrup
1 long peeled strip
    of lemon zest
20g butter
1 tablespoon coconut
    sugar or dark brown
    sugar
Sea salt

Preheat the oven to 150°C (130°C fan), gas mark 2, and put a roasting pan in to heat up.

Put the rice, milk, maple syrup, lemon zest and a pinch of salt into a saucepan and bring to a simmer, then leave to bubble very gently for a good 20 minutes.

Pour the mixture into the hot roasting pan, dot with butter and sprinkle over the sugar. Place in the oven for 20–30 minutes until the pudding has a golden brown top and is thick and creamy.

I would urge you to let the pudding sit for at least 15 minutes before serving. Add a spoonful of your favourite jam – gooseberry or apricot are especially good to complement the maple syrup and lemon. It is also delicious with the marmalade baked pears (page 133).

TIP If you have all the time in the world you can put the rice, milk, maple syrup and lemon into a roasting pan in the preheated oven without simmering it first. You may think it will never thicken up: it will, but it can take up to 2½ hours, or longer if you use brown rice. After about 2 hours, when the rice has started to absorb the milk, dot on the butter and sprinkle over the sugar.

LUMBERJACK FLAPJACK

I came across lumberjack cake in New Zealand and thought it would make a great hybrid with flapjack, with an oaty fruity base and a coconutty top. I usually make this with gluten-free oats and flour.

SERVES 6–8

4 eating apples, skin on –
   2 coarsely grated;
   2 quartered, cored and
   sliced into half moons
360g oats
100g soft light
   brown sugar
60g plain flour
200g butter, melted
Sea salt

**FOR THE LUMBERJACK
   TOPPING**
150g soft dark brown
   sugar or coconut sugar,
   or a mixture of both
150g butter, melted
130g flaked unsweetened
   coconut
375ml boiling milk

Preheat the oven to 180°C (160°C fan), gas mark 4. Line a small roasting pan (approx. 30 x 20cm) with a reusable silicone baking sheet.

Mix the grated apple, oats, sugar, flour and a pinch of salt together in a bowl. Pour in the melted butter and stir until the mixture comes together. Press into the lined pan and bake until golden, about 20 minutes.

While the base is baking, make the lumberjack topping by mixing all the ingredients together.

Scatter the sliced apples over the flapjack and then pour over the lumberjack mixture. Bake for another 15–20 minutes until the top is golden and set.

Serve hot as a pudding or leave to cool to enjoy with coffee, in a lunchbox or at teatime.

MARMALADE BAKED PEARS

These pears are so easy to do and are lovely as a pudding with some cream or custard and a ginger biscuit, or to go on top of porridge. They will keep for several days in the fridge, so are well worth doing.

SERVES 4

VEGAN

3 tablespoons marmalade
2 teaspoons ground
  ginger
300ml boiling water
4 pears, peeled and cut in
  half, no need to core

Preheat the oven to 150°C (130°C fan), gas mark 2.

Mix the marmalade and ginger together and stir into the boiling water. Put the pears, core-side down, into a roasting pan. Pour in the hot liquid, cover with foil and cook for 30–40 minutes until the pears are soft. Remove the foil for the last 15 minutes to thicken the sauce a little.

If you want more of a glaze than a sauce, you can lift out the pears, turn the oven up to 200°C (180°C fan), gas mark 2, and let the sauce reduce slightly, stirring regularly. Serve hot or leave to cool before storing in the fridge.

BAKED RHUBARB, ROSE WATER AND PINK GRAPEFRUIT

Baked rhubarb is wonderful with rice pudding or porridge, or as a fool made with cream and yoghurt. I also use it in the rhubarb, pistachio and ginger cake on page 136.

SERVES 4–6

VEGAN

1 pink grapefruit
1kg rhubarb, cut into
  5cm lengths
200g unrefined
  caster sugar
1 teaspoon rose water

Preheat the oven to 150°C (130°C fan), gas mark 2.

Using a vegetable peeler, peel off a couple of strips of zest from the pink grapefruit and set aside. Cut the grapefruit in half and squeeze the juice into a bowl, adding some of the pulpy flesh.

Toss the rhubarb with the sugar, grapefruit and rose water. Put everything into a roasting pan and cover with foil. Place in the oven and cook for 20 minutes, stir and continue to cook until the rhubarb is very tender but still has its shape – this will probably take another 20 minutes. Outdoor-grown rhubarb often collapses more, but don't worry, it will be delicious anyway.

TIP This is a lovely way of cooking rhubarb, especially early in the season when you can buy forced rhubarb – it will end up with the most glorious pink colour. As the season goes on you'll find outdoor-grown rhubarb, which is slightly more tart and not so vibrant in colour. The amount of sugar I have suggested is for outdoor rhubarb, so you may want to cut it back if you are lucky enough to get early forced rhubarb.

RHUBARB, PISTACHIO AND GINGER CAKE

This recipe is inspired by one from my favourite cookbook, Margaret Costa's Four Seasons Cookery Book. *She calls it orange snow cake and says it doesn't need icing as it is lovely and moist and keeps very well.*

SERVES 6

175g butter, softened, plus extra for greasing
150g unrefined caster sugar
2 eggs, separated
280g self-raising flour
2 heaped tablespoons baked rhubarb (page 134), or rhubarb jam or honey
55g crystallised ginger, chopped into small confetti-sized pieces
85g pistachios, finely chopped
5 tablespoons rhubarb juice reserved from cooking the rhubarb, or water
Sea salt

Preheat the oven to 180°C (160°C fan), gas mark 4. Butter a small (30 x 20cm) roasting pan.

Gradually beat the sugar into the butter until light and fluffy. Beat in the egg yolks, one at a time, adding a little flour to keep the mixture stable.

Stir in the rhubarb, ginger, pistachios and rhubarb juice or water and mix thoroughly.

Beat the egg whites with a pinch of salt until stiff. Gently fold the flour into the cake mixture and then fold in one-third of the egg whites and combine very well. Carefully fold in the remaining egg whites, ensuring everything is very well mixed and taking care to keep it as light as possible. Turn the mixture into the roasting pan and bake for 45 minutes.

Test by inserting a thin skewer or a piece of spaghetti into the centre of the cake. It should come out easily and perfectly clean. Leave to cool before turning out on a plate.

RASPBERRY AND SOUR CREAM SQUARES

This recipe works well with many other fruits, such as blueberries, sliced peaches, apricots or plums, quartered figs and – in winter – prunes, but is especially delicious with raspberries and very hard to resist.

SERVES 6–8

FOR THE BASE
250g plain flour
70g icing sugar
225g butter, melted
Sea salt

FOR THE TOPPING
3 eggs
100g unrefined caster
  sugar
3 tablespoons cornflour
Seeds scraped from ½ a
  vanilla pod
225g sour cream
300g raspberries

Preheat the oven to 180°C (160°C fan), gas mark 4. Line a small roasting pan (approx. 30 x 20cm) with a reusable silicone baking sheet.

Mix the flour, icing sugar, butter and salt together and press into the base of the pan in an even layer. Bake for about 15 minutes until golden.

While the base is cooking, prepare the topping. Whisk the eggs, sugar, cornflour and vanilla together until completely smooth. Gradually stir in the sour cream until fully combined.

Turn the oven down to 150°C (130°C fan), gas mark 2.

Pour the egg mixture over the hot base and scatter over the raspberries. Return to the oven for about 30 minutes until the top is set – you may want to turn the pan once during cooking to ensure it cooks evenly.

Leave on a wire rack to cool before cutting into squares. The first one may be tricky to remove but that's the cooks reward!

CHESTNUT, ORANGE AND CHOCOLATE BREAD PUDDING

Bread pudding is traditional English fare – but this is an updated version,
with chestnut purée, fresh orange and cocoa and some dark chocolate melted on top.

SERVES 4–6

50g butter, coarsely
grated, plus extra
for greasing

250g bread – use any
type you like

3 oranges

200g chestnut purée

65g dark brown sugar

1 egg

1 teaspoon vanilla extract

1 tablespoon cocoa
powder

20g dark chocolate,
roughly grated or
chopped

1–2 teaspoons demerara
sugar

Preheat the oven to 180°C (160°C fan), gas mark 4. Butter a roasting pan
(approx. 35 x 25cm).

Soak the bread in water until it is soft and disintegrating.

Meanwhile, grate the zest of one orange and set aside. Using a sharp
knife, cut off the peel and pith from all three oranges, then separate the
segments, catching any juice.

Lift the bread out of the water and give it a good squeeze. Put it in a bowl
with the butter, chestnut purée, brown sugar, egg, vanilla, cocoa, orange
zest and any juice. Mix everything thoroughly with a wooden spoon until
you have a silky mass. Fold in the orange segments then tip the mixture
into the roasting pan and level it out.

Sprinkle over the dark chocolate and the demerara sugar and bake for
45 minutes until just set. It will seem slightly wobbly when hot, but it will
become firmer as it cools. I like to serve it warm with double cream or
crème fraîche – or custard for comfort!

WALNUT, PECAN AND DATE SQUARES

This is my take on pecan pie. The dates make a lovely rich top: I added the eggs to make it a little lighter, but you can omit them to make an excellent vegan pud. It is also gluten free.

SERVES 8–10

75g ground almonds
75g walnuts, finely
   chopped
50g ground rice
100g cornflour
70g icing sugar
100g almond butter
50ml boiling water
Sea salt

FOR THE TOPPING
250g dates
150ml coffee
1 teaspoon vanilla extract
80g walnuts
2 eggs
125g pecans

Preheat the oven to 180°C (160°C fan), gas mark 4. Line a small roasting pan (approx. 30 x 20cm) with a reusable silicone baking sheet.

Mix the almonds, walnuts, ground rice and a pinch of salt together and sift in the cornflour and the icing sugar. In a jug, mix the almond butter with the hot water. Make a well in the centre of the dry ingredients and pour in the hot liquid. Gradually mix in the dry ingredients until it comes together like a slightly wet dough. Put it into the roasting pan and press it out to the corners, using your slightly dampened hands or the back of a spoon to level out the dough. Bake for 15 minutes until light brown and set.

Meanwhile, put the dates in a saucepan with the coffee and simmer until they are very soft and the coffee has reduced slightly. Leave to cool, then put into a food processor with the vanilla and walnuts and whizz to a paste. Add the eggs, one by one, with the motor running. Tip the date mixture over the base and scatter the pecans over. Bake for 20 minutes until the top is set. Serve warm or leave on a wire rack to cool to make it easier to cut into squares.

APRICOT AND PISTACHIO TART

Fresh apricots are a delicious treat in early summer. They look beautiful in this tart,
with its fragrant filling based on a Turkish milk pudding.

SERVES 6

Approx 500g ready-made
  sweet shortcrust pastry
500ml whole milk
50g ground pistachios,
  plus an extra
  15g pistachios, roughly
  chopped, to serve
30g ground almonds
35g ground rice
100ml single cream
50g golden caster sugar
Few drops of rose water
12 apricots, halved
  and stoned
5 tablespoons vanilla
  sugar
Small nut of butter
2 tablespoons apple juice,
  cider or rosé wine
Sea salt

Preheat the oven to 200°C (180°C fan), gas mark 6. On a lightly floured surface, roll out the pastry to about 3mm thick, then use it to line a small roasting pan (approx. 30 x 20cm). Trim off any excess, then line the pastry with a reusable silicone baking sheet. Fill with baking beans or rice, then blind bake the pastry case for 20 minutes. Carefully remove the parchment and beans and bake for another 5 minutes until the pastry is cooked through.

Scald 150ml of the milk and pour it into a food processor with the ground nuts. Whizz for 20 seconds.

Mix together the ground rice, cream and a pinch of salt. Heat the remaining milk in a saucepan and bring to a simmer, then add the ground rice mixture and cook, stirring, for a couple of minutes until thickened. Now add the ground nut mix and the sugar and continue to simmer until the mixture thickens.

Remove from the heat and beat in the rose water. Pour into the cooked pastry case and gently spread out in an even layer. It will solidify as it cools.

Turn the oven up to 220°C (200°C fan), gas mark 7. Place the apricots in a roasting pan, cut-side up, sprinkle over the vanilla sugar and dot over the butter. Sprinkle the juice, cider or wine around the fruit. Bake for 20–25 minutes until the apricots are just soft, with some syrupy juices. Arrange the fruit on top of the tart filling and brush with the juices to glaze. Scatter over the chopped pistachios.

INDEX

ACKNOWLEDGEMENTS

A recipe book always requires plenty of collaboration and this one is no exception. So here is my roll call of gratitude and recognition.

Many thanks Helen Lewis, excellent creative director at Pavilion and Gemma Doyle, design manager, and the fantastic photo team: Dan Jones image-capturer extraordinaire and his assistant, India Whiley-Morton. The incredible cooks and stylists Rosie Ramsden (fellow sausage dog owner – extra kudos there) and Rosie French, along with Davina Perkins and her gorgeous props. Also thank you to those foresighted people at Pavilion: Polly Powell for your initial interest and Peter Taylor and the National Trust thereafter. Thanks Kristy Richardson for your support and Maggie Ramsay for making sense of my recipes. And of course eternal gratitude to my agent Victoria Hobbs who is endlessly encouraging.

Thanks to the friends who inspire me in the world of food: Laura Jackson for her amazing Towpath kitchen, where I always feel excited and inspired to cook with her marvellous team – with Lori de Mori a big part of that joy. Leila McAlister, whose shop and general wonderfulness constantly hearten. Joyce Molyneux, Shaun Hill and Juliet Peston my most eminent head chefs, still behind me when I cook. Tim Dillon, Karl Goward, Kevin Mcfadden, Steve Williams, Adam Sellar, James Ferguson, Jack Van Praag, Lucas Hollweg all stellar chefs with whom I have worked, learnt and laughed. Pauline Griffiths whose wonderful sense of style has helped me hone my craft and William Griffiths and Emily Heath, always nearby. I am fortunate to have a tiptoe in the food writer fraternity – a source of ongoing inspiration – my very favourites whom I call friends too: Rachel Roddy, Claire Thomson, Sarit Packer, Itamar Srulovich, Jenny Linford along with Patricia Niven – amazing photographer – and my surrogate brother and pensmith Bob Granleese. Heidi White, a powerhouse of the Cambridge food scene. Duncan Catchpole, a visionary food pioneer, Tyler Cotton a brilliant grower and Kenneth Mackay who is helping me set up my own veg patch. Finally Barny Haughton, founder and force behind the Square Food Foundation, a deeply inspiring individual who, among many other things, has helped me to see a future in the food world and beyond.

So to the nearest and dearest who test, taste, correct and encourage: My sisters Annabel and Camilla and their families. Polly Russell a dear, dear friend and most excellent cook – she and her family are super guinea pigs thanks Steve, Milly, Trixie and godson George. My co-pilot, great friend and very good cook Thomas Blythe (see Tom's Sausages and Beans, page 28). Claire Roberson, always there with wise words and laughter. Eric Ssewagudde, top buddy and appreciative taster. George Perry, dear friend with generous reading and writing wisdom. Countless more to mention including: Sam Walker, George Sinclair, Lucie Reeder, Jacq Burns, Ana Garcia, Kate Brewin, Aunty Mary and my lovely neighbours Andrea, Alan and Amy.

I have had two untimely losses in the past years who are always with me – great cooks themselves, we spent a lot of our times together talking about food, preparing it, cooking it and eating it. Thank you Dad and my brother Chris – you are both still part of what I create in the kitchen.

My life has two constants, to whom I would like to dedicate this book: one is my very, very dearest and closest friend Imogen who is so clever and full of ideas and helps and supports me endlessly – I would be lost without you. The same goes for the sausage dog (she lives with me but I hesitate to claim ownership she is very much her own dog!) Florence Salome, she is the most heartwarming creature one could hope for with so much pluck and spirit – a steadfast companion.